# SUMMING UP

# SUMMING UP

## THE SCIENCE OF REVIEWING RESEARCH

RICHARD J. LIGHT

DAVID B. PILLEMER

Harvard University Press

Cambridge, Massachusetts, and London, England   1984

LIBRARY OF CONGRESS CATALOGING IN PUBLICATION DATA

Light, Richard J.
    Summing up.

    Bibliography: p.
    Includes index.
    1. Social sciences—Research.    2. Social sciences—
Bibliography—Methodology.    I.  Pillemer, David B.,
1950-   .   II.  Title.
H62.L46   1984        300'.72        84-4506
ISBN 0-674-85430-6 (alk. paper) (cloth)
ISBN 0-674-85431-4 (paper)

# CONTENTS

## PREFACE

We decided to write this book because of persistent questions about how to strengthen new research. Each of us has been sought out by others for help in designing new investigations. These requests have come from public agencies and decision-makers as well as academic colleagues and students. And although the details of the questions change, the broad outlines are extraordinarily similar.

The dialogue begins with a request for help in designing a study. We then ask what has been learned in that particular subject area from earlier studies. After all, new investigations should build upon existing knowledge. The response, nearly always, is that the group of earlier studies is complex and even contradictory. Indeed, the contradictions are an important reason for conducting a new study.

Our questioners seldom consider investing time and resources to synthesize the information that already exists. We wondered why not. This seems to be a sensible first step. Without a clear picture of where things now stand, simply adding one new study to the existing morass is unlikely to be very useful.

Scientists are not the only ones who ask questions about "what research adds up to." Policymakers must make practical decisions based on what is known *now*. In the early 1970s Walter Mondale, then a Senator, in an address to the American Educational Research Association, spoke about research on racial integration in America's public schools: "What I have not learned is what we should do about these problems. I had hoped to find research to support or to conclusively oppose my belief that quality integrated education is the most promising approach. But I have found very little conclusive evidence. For every study, statistical or theoretical, that contains a proposed solution or recommendation, there is always another, equally well documented, challenging the assumptions or conclusions of the first. No one seems to agree with anyone else's approach. But more distressing: no one seems to know what works. As a result, I must confess, I stand with my colleagues confused and often disheartened."

The frustration Mr. Mondale expressed is both widespread and understandable. He wants some firm information, whether it comes down on one side or the other, and he cannot find it. His description of the lack of consistency in scientific findings unfortunately applies not only to research on racial integration but to many other issues as well.

Apart from the formulation of policy, difficulties in reconciling contradictory conclusions from similar studies cripple a fundamental component of the scientific process: the systematic accumulation of knowledge. Mark Twain said in his autobiography, "The thirteenth stroke of a clock is not only false of itself, but casts grave doubts on the credibility of the preceding twelve." This statement captures a critical part of the experience of doing applied research. It seems that for every twelve studies reaching any specific conclusion there is always a thirteenth that disagrees. Mark Twain's solution might well have been to put all thirteen behind him and light out for the Territories. The equivalent of this action in research would be to discard the conflicting evidence and initiate a new study. But such a step would incur three costs: a great deal of information, some potentially valuable, would be thrown away; a decision would be postponed for at least the length of time the new research takes; and, from the point of view of the next reviewer of the literature, the new research would simply be the fourteenth in the set of studies. Even with difficult problems, it is worth trying to combine and reconcile conflicting outcomes.

Clearly, society must improve its efforts to learn from existing findings, to "discover what is known." In this spirit we began a search for procedures, accessible to nonstatisticians, that would enhance the scientific quality of research summaries. We examined what reviewers currently do when they tackle a group of studies done by different people in different places at different times. Our search led ultimately to the writing of this book. In it we present circumstances under which it makes sense to use various statistical techniques. We suggest new ways of using simple graphical displays to examine patterns among findings. We emphasize conceptual issues throughout, because carefully planned reviews are nearly always stronger and more useful than atheoretical foraging. We also provide strategies for using different kinds of information from many studies. Some studies are primarily numerical; others are narrative or qualitative. Some have large sample sizes; others are tiny. Some have controlled research designs; othes do not. Our broad goal is to help readers organize existing evidence in a systematic way, whether a review is motivated by a scientific problem or the need for a policy decision. The book should also help readers examine and evaluate reviews prepared by others.

Our suggestions apply to many fields, including education, health, psychology, and policy sciences, and we include illustrations from each. We have tried to write at a technical level accessible to a broad audience, including academic researchers, policy analysts, and students beginning their careers. We hope this book will help them to strengthen connections between current research and accumulated knowledge from the past.

## ACKNOWLEDGMENTS

We both have many thanks to offer. A grant from the Spencer Foundation greatly facilitated our effort. H. Thomas James, President of the Spencer Foundation, has been supportive for years. We have benefited from conversations about research reviews with Robert F. Boruch, Eleanor Chelimsky, Thomas D. Cook, David S. Cordray, Gene V. Glass, Larry V. Hedges, Linda Morra, Robert Rosenthal, Michael A. Stoto, Herbert J. Walberg, and Sheldon H. White. We especially would like to acknowledge detailed comments on earlier drafts of this manuscript from Anthony S. Bryk, Robert E. Klitgaard, Frederick Mosteller, Stephen W. Raudenbush, Paul V. Smith, Terrence Tivnan, and Eric Wanner. Alicia Schrier helped with computer simulations and analyses, and William Minty prepared figures and charts. Camille Smith's superb editing improved the manuscript substantially.

Each of us has additional acknowledgments. Thanks to the generosity of Wellesley College, David Pillemer received a year's leave from teaching to work on this book; he spent the year as a Visiting Scholar in the Department of Psychology and Social Relations, Harvard University. Richard Light has benefited from working with the staff of the Program Evaluation and Methodology Division of the General Accounting Office. As chairman of a National Academy of Sciences panel on evaluating children's programs, funded by the Carnegie Corporation, he learned a great deal about research reviews in education. His wife, Pat, and daughters, Jennifer and Sarah, provided the greatest support of all.

We are grateful for permission to use the following illustrative materials in this book. Box 1.2: editorial by permission of *The Washington Post,* copyright © 1982 by *The Washington Post;* letter from George D. Wilson by permission of George D. Wilson and the American Meat Institute. Table 2.1 by permission from J. M. Lachlin, N. Tygstrup, and E. Juhl, eds., *The Randomized Clinical Trial and Therapeutic Decisions* (New York: Marcel Dekker, 1982). Box 3.2: Figure A by permission from *Annual Review of Nuclear Science,* 25 (1975), copyright © 1975 by Annual Reviews Inc. Figure 3.4 by permission from C. C. Kulik and J. A. Kulik, "Effects of ability grouping on secondary school students: a meta-analysis of evaluation findings," *American Educational Research Journal,* 19 (1982), copyright © 1982 by the American Educational Research Association, Washington, D.C. Figure 3.14 by permission from G. V. Glass, "Integrating findings: a meta-analysis of research," *Review of Research in Education,* 5 (1977), copyright © 1977 by the American Educational Research Association. Figure 3.15 by permission from R. E. Klitgaard and G. Hall, *A Statistical Search for Unusually Effective Schools* (Santa Monica, Calif.: Rand, 1973), copyright © 1973 by the Rand Corporation. Figure 4.2 by permission from R. J. Light and David B. Pillemer, "Numbers and narrative: combining their strengths in research reviews," *Harvard Educa-*

ACKNOWLEDGMENTS

*tional Review,* 52 (1982). Box 5.1: Figure B by permission from G. V. Glass and M. L. Smith, "Meta-analysis of research on class size achievement," *Educational Evaluation and Policy Analysis,* 1 (1979), copyright © 1979 by the American Educational Research Association.

# SUMMING UP

# 1

A professor is called to testify before Congress as to whether a program offering nutritional supplements to low-income pregnant women should be expanded. Do the supplements improve maternal health? Do they improve child health?

A policymaker faces the challenge of restructuring the parole board system in a state. Are changes necessary? What changes would be most constructive?

An ambitious graduate student wants to try out an innovative housing program for elderly citizens. The plan is to have residents make decisions collectively. Are participants happier and healthier as a result?

Each of these people would benefit enormously by pausing before taking action and asking a few questions: What is known about the magnitude of the problem? What efforts have been made in the past to ameliorate it? Were they successful? Does existing evidence suggest any promising new directions? These questions demand some way to formalize "what we already know."

Where can one turn for answers? Consider the graduate student and his housing innovation. Knowing that a good review of existing research should precede fieldwork, he approaches his faculty adviser for guidance. How does a scientist conduct a research review? What are the essential steps?

It is easy to imagine the student being slightly embarrassed to ask these questions, and the adviser feeling mild annoyance. Reviewing the literature is something a competent young scholar *should* know how to do. The professor's first reaction is likely to be that while the procedures are not carved in stone, some are quite standard. Go to the library. Use the social science abstracts. Thumb through current journals. Identify relevant articles. Briefly summarize them and draw some coherent overall conclusions.

Yet if the faculty member is pressed to give *explicit* guidelines, her annoyance may turn to frustration. How can relevant articles be identified? Which of tens or hundreds of studies of programs for the elderly should a summary present? How should conflicting findings from different studies be resolved? Trying to answer these questions may make it clear that the professor's "scientific" procedures are implicit rather than explicit, as much art as science.

Feeling this frustration, the faculty adviser takes the offensive. The absence of formal reviewing procedures is an inconvenience, but this does not undermine the research process. *New* research is the basis of scientific achievement. A research review is a chore to dispose of as quickly and painlessly as possible, usually by delegating it to subordinates. The student meekly replies that his *new* research will soon be somebody else's *old* data, receiving short shrift in a review article. But the lesson has been passed on to a new generation of scientists.

Why do scientists think that new research is better, or

more insightful, or more powerful? The underlying assumption must be that new studies will incorporate and improve upon lessons learned from earlier work. Novelty in and of itself is shallow without links to the past. It is possible to evaluate an innovation only by comparisons with its predecessors.

For science to be cumulative, an intermediate step between past and future research is necessary: synthesis of existing evidence. The casual attitude of some scientists toward this step undermines the value of many new research initiatives. With tens of studies examining questions such as the effectiveness of Head Start, the value of heart bypass graft surgery, or the impact of television advertising directed to young children, producing a useful summary requires systematic methods. Studies are done by different people, at different places, at different times. They may use different outcome measures, research designs, and analysis formats. The number and diversity of studies challenge even an expert's ability to "pull it all together" without formal tools.

## Current Status of the Research Review

For many years, the "literature review" has been a routine step along the way to presenting a new study or laying the groundwork for an innovation. Journals such as *Psychological Bulletin, Review of Educational Research, American Public Health Journal,* and *New England Journal of Medicine* publish the best of such reviews. Traditionally, these efforts to accumulate information have been unsystematic. Studies are presented in serial fashion, with strengths and weaknesses discussed selectively and informally. These informal reviews often have several shortcomings:

1. The traditional review is *subjective.* Since the process has few formal rules, two well-intentioned reviewers can disagree about issues as basic as what studies to include and how to resolve conflicts between studies. The result is that rather than organizing diverse outcomes into a set of reason-

ably conclusive findings, the reviews themselves are open to attack for including inappropriate or poorly done studies or for drawing conclusions subjectively. Instead of resolving conflicts among the various studies, the review may only generate new conflicts.

2. The traditional review is *scientifically unsound*. Without formal guidelines, a reviewer may reach conclusions using methods inconsistent with good statistical practice. For example, when some studies show a positive program effect while others show no relationship or even a negative effect, a common way to summarize these findings is to use a "vote count." A reviewer counts up the number of studies supporting various sides of an issue and chooses the view receiving the most "votes." This procedure ignores sample size, effect size, and research design. Serious errors can result (Hedges and Olkin, 1980; Light and Smith, 1971).

3. The traditional review is an *inefficient way to extract useful information*. This is especially true when the number of studies is large, perhaps thirty or more. A reviewer unarmed with formal tools to extract and summarize findings must rely on an extraordinary ability to mentally juggle relationships among many variables. Systematic ways of exploring such relationships would make it far easier both to detect and to understand them. (Box 1.1 gives an illustration of the difficult issues facing narrative reviewers.)

One contemporary response to these shortcomings is to use statistical procedures for combining findings. Excellent books presenting quantitative methods include Glass, McGaw, and Smith (1981) and Hunter, Schmidt, and Jackson (1982). Quantitative procedures appeal to the wish for a sense of order that a complex body of findings can generate. We present some of these techniques in the chapters that follow. But our focus is on broader questions. How does one *structure* a research review? How does one even *think* about different ways of aggregating information? What *qualitative* sources of information are especially valuable?

**BOX 1.1.  CONFLICTS BETWEEN NARRATIVE REVIEWS**

For years scientists have debated the extent to which schools and home environments influence children's IQ test scores. One way of assessing this impact is to examine the cognitive performance of adopted children. Munsinger (1974) examined a group of adoption studies and concluded that environmental effects are small: "Available data suggest that under existing circumstances heredity is much more important than environment in producing individual differences in IQ" (p. 623). Kamin (1978) later reviewed the *same* group of studies and reached the opposite conclusion.

That two distinguished scientists interpret a set of results so differently is only slightly surprising, since the personal beliefs of a reviewer can play a role in resolving disparate findings. This is especially true for a topic as controversial as nature-nurture. Far more striking are their different views on what constitutes acceptable review standards. According to Kamin, "Munsinger's review of the adoption literature is in general unreliable. Though any review must be selective in its presentation and analysis of data, Munsinger's is excessively so" (p. 194). Munsinger (1978) replies: "Kamin accuses me of errors and selective reporting of the adoption data, but in fact Kamin's comments are quite selective and often incorrect" (p. 202). These conflicting views about evidence are particularly apparent in comments on a study by Freeman, Holzinger, and Mitchell (1928): Kamin describes it as "large-scale and extraordinarily interesting" (p. 200); Munsinger argues that it is "replete with methodological and statistical difficulties" (1974, p. 635).

Kamin (1978) concludes: "perhaps the major point to be made is that readers interested in evaluating the evidence on heritability of IQ ought not to depend on published summaries. Those who wish to speak or to teach accurately about what is and is not known have no realistic alternative but to read the literature themselves" (p. 200). Taken literally, this statement eliminates the review as a scientific or practical tool. It is not practical to expect all people interested in a medical treatment, or a Head Start program, or even an issue as complicated as environmental impact on IQ, to read dozens of original scientific studies. Surely it is worth trying to develop systematic procedures for summarizing the literature. If two reviewers using explicit procedures reach different conclusions, at least readers can see why and then make an informed choice.

The science of preparing reviews has experienced a revolution of sorts in recent years. But the fruits of this work have not yet entered into the training of most social scientists, educators, and policymakers. For example, Jackson (1980) reports that *none* of a sample of 39 books on general methodology in social science devotes more than two pages to literature reviews. Jackson's investigation of the quality of social science reviews published in the period 1970–1976 turned up an almost complete lack of systematic procedures. Most contemporary reviews are still informal and discursive.

For social science to get the maximum benefit from prior research, sound reviewing strategies must become more accessible, more highly valued, and a routine part of advanced undergraduate and graduate training. We have designed this book as a small contribution toward these goals. (Box 1.2 presents a public debate about the value of synthesis.)

---

**BOX 1.2. COMMISSIONING A NEW STUDY VERSUS SYNTHESIZING AVAILABLE EVIDENCE**

In mid 1982 the National Academy of Sciences issued a long-awaited report on the link between diet and cancer. Part of this report described the research tying consumption of different kinds of meat to the likelihood of developing cancer. On June 19, 1982, the *Washington Post* published an editorial entitled "Food and Cancer," which said in part:

If you are one of those people who have just about given up on making sense of the conflicting medical advice about what to eat, help—at least of a kind—is on the way. A striking convergence of expert opinion is coming about. More and more evidence shows that diet strongly influences the risk of coronary heart disease, cancer, hypertension and other major killers. And the recommended changes in diet for lowering the risk of each of these diseases reinforce, rather than contradict, each other.

The newest evidence comes from a two-year study of the connections between diet and cancer, issued this week by the National Academy of Sciences. The group found first of all that research into this vast and complex subject has hardly scratched the surface. But it did find enough persuasive evidence to justify issuing what it called four "interim dietary guidelines"—the first and last words indicating that the evidence is not complete and that these are not absolute rules that will guarantee a cancer-free life.

But in the committee's judgment, following the guidelines will lower the risk of getting cancer. And since diet (not including smoking) is believed to be responsible for at least 30–40 percent of cancers, that should be enough to command attention.

The committee recommends that people restrict their intake of fats—saturated *and* unsaturated—to 30 percent of total calories. For the average American, that means cutting fat consumption—such things as whole milk and its products, ice cream, peanut butter, cooking fats and oils, beef and other fatty meats—by one quarter. The committee also recommends eating "very little salt-cured, salt-pickled, or smoked foods," which include ham, bacon, bologna and hot dogs . . .

There will be criticism of these recommendations on the ground that the experimental evidence is not conclusive. But as the Academy's report points out, "we are in an interim stage of knowledge similar to that for cigarettes 20 years ago." (Cigarettes are causing one-quarter of the cancer deaths today.) Since absolutely conclusive evidence will take years to develop, the committee members felt that the evidence justifies action now. Surely they are right.

On July 3, 1982, the *Post* published a letter from George D. Wilson, Vice President for Scientific Affairs of the American Meat Institute. In his response to the June 19 editorial he was concerned about seeming contradictions in the reported results of different reviews of the impact of nitrites and cured meats on health. He said in part:

Contrary to the bold conclusions set forth in the report of this NAS committee, both the National Research Council and the Food and Nutrition Board of the National Academy of Sciences having engaged in extensive evaluations of the potential health implications of fat and nitrite consumption, have published statements in total disagreement with last week's announcement.

There should be a real concern that a committee clothed with the credibility of the National Academy of Sciences would make unequivocal and drastic dietary recommendations on the basis of inconclusive evidence which only adds to consumer confusion and uncertainty.

On July 15 the *Post* published a letter from Wendell Bailey, a Republican member of the House of Representatives from Missouri. Under the heading "Not One Scintilla of New Research," his letter said in part:

> The *Post* has given considerable attention to the recent report "Diet, Nutrition and Cancer" by the National Research Council, done as part of a $950,583 three-year National Cancer Institute grant that wasn't even put up for bid.
>
> But . . . the "study" offers no new evidence . . . it is merely a survey of already-published documents that, if they were newsworthy, would have been sought out by your enterprising reporters even if the studies had been originally published in scholarly tomes. Someone would have said, "Look at this medical breakthrough on cancer."
>
> . . . The scientists wrapped their "old fish" in a new "study" and permitted it to be dumped as news, with no concern for its impact on the lives of countless millions of Americans, economically or health-wise.
>
> Paul L. Sitton, assistant to the president of the NAS, concedes that NAS has no laboratories and has done no experimental work on the relationship of meat to cancer. Despite this, the NAS feels sufficiently persuaded to issue a statement that bullyrags the red-meat industry and shouts "wolf" at diet- and health-conscious Americans—a statement that urges the public to consume less meat, yet provides not one scintilla of new research to support the recommendations.

Representative Bailey puts the question sharply. In a debate such as this, which spills over traditional scientific borders into the arena of public policy, we should ask what would in fact have been more valuable: spending the $950,000 to collect new data for a 101st study to add to the already existing 100, or commissioning a review, using the same $950,000, to learn as much as possible from the many studies already available?

## Four Themes

In this book we develop four general themes. The first is that any reviewing strategy must come from the precise questions driving the review. It is helpful to approach a review with structure. Structure is provided by clearly specifying a review's purpose. Is an overall answer desirable, or is the purpose to identify setting-by-treatment interactions? Is the goal to influence policy or to refine further research? The answers to these questions should guide the selection of analytic techniques. Many reviews do not build on this initial organization. The result is often a simple taxonomy of findings, doing little to help either policy or future research.

Our second theme is that disagreements among findings are valuable and should be exploited. When faced with dozens of studies of, say, Head Start, it is natural to hope most of the findings will agree. When they do, integrating them is usually easy and uncontroversial. But this rarely happens. Jackson (1980) found that most literature reviews report conflicting outcomes.

When study outcomes disagree, it is tempting to throw up one's hands and assume the research is useless. We believe just the opposite: such conflicts can teach us a lot. Looked at positively, they actually offer an *opportunity* to examine and learn about divergent findings. There usually are several potential explanations. There may be substantive differences between treatments with the same name. Or perhaps a program works well in certain settings and poorly in others. Exploring the reasons for conflicting outcomes can tell us where a program is likely to succeed in the future.

The third theme is that both numerical and qualitative information play key roles in a good synthesis. Quantitative procedures appeal to scientists and policymakers who experience feelings of futility when trying to develop a clear statement of "what is known." But using them does not reduce the value of careful program descriptions, case studies, narrative reports, or expert judgment, even though this information may be difficult to quantify. We cannot afford to ignore any information that may provide solid answers. For most purposes, a review using both numerical and narrative information will outperform its one-sided counterparts. For example, formal statistical analysis is often needed to identify small effects across studies that are not apparent through casual inspection (Cooper and Rosenthal, 1980). But qualitative analyses of program characteristics are necessary to explain the effect and to decide whether it matters for policy.

Our fourth theme is that statistical precision cannot substitute for conceptual clarity. We do not offer a set of rigid guidelines for doing reviews, nor would this be desirable. Preparing a review is too often a purely empirical or mechanical enterprise. A simple tally of research outcomes leaves many questions unanswered. When are different techniques appropriate? Why are they valuable? How might they be improved? These questions are complex and not easily resolved. Yet we believe it is helpful to examine how specific reviews and reviewing procedures lead to broader scientific progress.

## Organization of the Book

The chapters of this book build upon one another, but each can be read separately. A reader especially interested in a particular topic can profit from looking at only the chapter on that topic.

Chapter 2 details several organizational issues that a reviewer must resolve before plunging in. These include identifying a focal question, choosing studies, deciding if the venture is exploratory or hypothesis-testing, determining the potential generalizability of results, and building in a way to exploit differences among studies. It is hard to imagine any well-done review that overlooks these issues.

Chapter 3 gets to the nuts and bolts of doing reviews. Specific procedures are presented and evaluated. Topics include statistical techniques, special visual displays, analysis of exceptional outcomes ("outliers"), and several ways to explain conflicts among studies. We conclude with a discussion of special statistical problems, such as missing data.

Chapter 4 presents a rationale for including case studies and qualitative data in a review. Since such information is considered messy, reviewers may be tempted to ignore it. But this involves a great, often unacceptable cost. Understanding the special role of qualitative data in science is essential for clarifying its contribution to reviews. We argue that a useful division of labor exists between numbers and narrative, and we outline specific methods for combining their strengths in reviews.

Chapter 5 pays off the preceding sections. We discuss some exemplary reviews that illustrate how systematic procedures provide answers to real-world substantive questions. The examples cover a wide range of topics, including coronary bypass surgery, deinstitutionalization of mental health patients, methods of reading instruction, and the impact of television viewing on children's performance in school. They nail down substantive findings, resolve controversies, and deliver broad lessons about scientific progress as of the 1980s. What have we learned? Does coaching students for standardized achievement tests offer substantial benefits? Is preventive health care for young children useful? Are the effects of most social programs small, medium, or large? We think most readers will encounter at least one or two surprises here.

Chapter 6 offers a checklist of ten questions general enough to ask of almost any review. They should be useful to consumers of reviews who wonder how convincing a set of conclusions are, and what questions should be asked. The checklist builds on the major lessons of the book. We suggest why each question is important and discuss the implications of different answers.

## ORGANIZING A REVIEWING STRATEGY

# 2

A crucial step in reviewing research is developing a guiding strategy. This step should not be overlooked. The nuts-and-bolts tasks that follow—statistical analysis and data presentation—are driven by the early organizational decisions. Five issues are at the heart of almost every review: (1) What specific question is the review trying to answer? (2) Is the review exploratory, or rather is it built around specific, testable hypotheses? (3) Which studies should be included? (4) To what population can the main findings be generalized? (5) Are there important differences in the ways studies were done?

These five issues motivate this chapter. It is hard to imagine a good review that ignores them. It is also hard to conceive of a set of unalterable rules for answering them. The issues are conceptual rather than technical. So there is no simple formula a reviewer can go to for "plug-in" solutions.

We believe the hard work of puzzling out answers will distinguish excellent reviews from their ordinary counterparts.

## Issue 1: Formulating a Precise Question

The first step in organizing a review is to specify its purpose. What precise question is the reviewer trying to answer? Far too many research reviews lack this initial direction entirely. Others begin with an overly broad question, such as "What do we know about a particular treatment?"

The example of the professor and student in Chapter 1 highlights a weakness of traditional ways of structuring reviews. The student's question, "How does one conduct a scientific review?," and the professor's effort to answer it imply that there is one generally agreed upon set of procedures. When discussing scientific reviews with colleagues we still sometimes hear, "Don't most people already know how to do *that*?" This view, that there is a single "that" for students to master, contributes to the problems we are addressing.

While there is no single "that," it is still essential to approach a review with structure. Structure is provided by clearly specifying the purpose of the enterprise. Think of a single study for a moment. When presenting findings from one study, there is little point in calculating elaborate statistics, or developing pages of process descriptions, unless the scientific purpose demands it. Reviews involving several studies are no different. The specific questions motivating a review should guide its preparation.

Reviews can answer many diverse questions. From our experience, three are most commonly asked by both scientists and policymakers:

What is the effect of a treatment *on average*?
*Where* and *with whom* is a treatment particularly effective or ineffective?
Will it work *here*? What are practical guidelines for implementing a treatment in a particular place?

We now suggest a general way to think about these questions.

### Structuring a Review: A Simple Functional Model

One way to express the questions a review might ask is to put them into functional form, such as

$$Y = f(T, X) + \text{Error.}$$

$Y$ represents an *outcome* of interest. The simplest situation is when that outcome has only one measure of success, such as length of life following surgery. Other situations may require multiple measures: blood pressure has both systolic and diastolic readings, for example, and the success of a job training program may be assessed by both income and job satisfaction.

$T$ represents a *treatment* of interest. The simplest situation compares one level of a treatment to a no-treatment control group. For example, did a person or hospital or city get special services or not? More complex situations also are common. Sometimes studies compare multiple treatments. This happens when there are several levels of one treatment (such as dosage of a drug, five mg versus ten mg or number of hours in a job training program, fifty versus two hundred), or when there are clearly different forms of a program (such as Montessori, Bereiter-Engelmann, and open classroom preschool curricula). The model also generalizes easily to comparisons between intact groups, such as males and females or low, medium, and high incomes, even though there is no experimental treatment in the formal sense.

$X$ represents *features of participants* that can influence research outcomes. For example, studies examining the effect of a drug might take into account the weight of the person taking it. Studies evaluating a job training program might look at the prior employment history and educational background of trainees.

The functional equation tells us that research outcomes, $Y$, depend upon both treatments, $T$, and participants, $X$, plus random error. We focus on $T$ and $X$ not because they are the only nonrandom influences—other characteristics of studies, such as type of research design, also can have an impact on demonstrated program effectiveness—but because they are key sources of variation in many reviews. We see that $X$, $T$, and $Y$ can all vary across studies, or even across different sites in a single study. It is useful, then, to tie $Y$, $T$, and $X$ and their functional format to different questions motivating a review.

One question is how $T$, a certain treatment, influences $Y$, the outcome, *on the average.* Does job training lead to higher average incomes? Answering this requires combining across different values of $T$, since it would be surprising if many studies of job training all examined the identical curriculum. It also requires averaging over different values of $X$, since trainees will differ from study to study.

A second question is whether *particular versions,* or implementations, of $T$ generally work better than others. Does a 10 mg dose of a drug work better for most recipients than a 5 mg dose? Does including a supplemental film in a presurgical information program lead to faster postoperative recovery than a class without the film? Answering this in a review requires comparing different values of $T$ and averaging across all values of $X$.

A different version of this question is whether *particular sorts of recipients* generally benefit more than others, and in predictable ways. Answering this requires averaging across different values of $T$, while comparing several specific $X$'s. Does a medication work best with patients who have a particular kind of heart problem, or does it benefit all cardiac patients equally? Does the effectiveness of a certain regimen for prisoners depend upon what kind of crime was committed, or on how long the criminal has yet to serve?

A refinement is more elegant but probably harder to answer: What *combination* of treatment and recipient is most, and least, effective? This is a "matching" question. It requires a reviewer to examine different combinations of $X$ and $T$. Is there a certain drug among several that is best matched to people who develop diabetes in their fifties as opposed to in childhood? This is more complex than the other questions, but it is also the one that can turn up the subtlest findings.

A third question is whether a treatment will work in a specific place. A job training program may be successful in many diverse locations. A city manager must still ask, "Will it work in *my* town—what is the evidence?" This requires matching a single treatment to one specific set of circumstances.

Each of these questions might motivate a research review. When is each particularly useful?

### What is the Average Effect of a Treatment?

It often is assumed that the purpose of a review is to "pull it all together." Translated into concrete terms, this implies estimating an average. Since reporting an "on average" finding requires sweeping generalizations covering an entire body of research, this question should be asked carefully. When is it the right question?

*Policy needs.* One function of a simple on-the-average summary is to meet policy needs. The real-world demands faced by policymakers are quite different from those confronting researchers (Rein and White, 1977). Academicians can be extremely cautious about generalizing research findings to policy settings. Policymakers necessarily operate under a different set of professional constraints. Decisions must be made. Programs must be implemented, funds spent and accounted for, clients served. This setting frequently demands *action*. For policymakers, a rigorous scientific summary of research can be a valuable supplement to political debate. (For an experienced policymaker's view, see Box 2.1.)

The needs of policymakers are sometimes well served by an overall on-the-average summary. Some policies are designed to affect different people rather indiscriminately. In these situations knowing the details of where or when a program works best is not as pressing as a more general evaluation.

The Federal Trade Commission's efforts to regulate television advertising directed to children illustrate this. In the late 1970s the FTC proposed rules to restrict children's exposure to ads in general and to commercials for heavily sugared products in particular (Adler et al., 1980). One of the proposed rules would have prohibited *all* advertising during TV shows viewed by substantial numbers of children under age eight.

Not surprisingly, these proposals sparked heated public and corporate reaction, both positive and negative. The de-

---

**BOX 2.1.  USING RESEARCH TO INFORM POLICY**

A former National Security Advisor has some interesting thoughts about relationships between research evidence and policy decisions. Kissinger (1960) points out that policy researchers must operate within a world of constraints set by others: "The contribution of the intellectual to policy is therefore in terms of criteria that he has played only a minor role in establishing. He is rarely given the opportunity to point out that a query limits a range of possible solutions or that an issue is posed in irrelevant terms. He is asked to solve problems, not to contribute to the definition of goals" (p. 350).

As to whether there is an abundance or shortage of research generally available to policymakers, Kissinger seems to believe the former: "The production of so much research often simply adds another burden to already overworked officials . . . Few if any of the recent crises of U.S. policy have been caused by the unavailability of data. Our policymakers do not lack in advice; they are in many respects overwhelmed by it" (p. 351).

Perhaps improved research reviews could reduce this feeling of being overwhelmed. Policymakers may not lack advice, but that advice could be enriched through clearer connections with existing scientific knowledge.

---

bate resulted in several lawsuits and contributed to an eventual limiting of the FTC's power by Congress. Reasons for opposition included weaknesses of research demonstrating negative effects of ads, antiregulatory sentiment, adverse reaction from the advertising industry, and arguments that parents are capable of controlling their children's viewing and purchasing behavior.

Our interest here is not in the specifics of the debate but in the potential role of research. There exists a substantial literature on the effects of TV ads on children (Adler et al., 1980). The strictest rule proposed by the FTC limits *all* TV advertising to *all* young children, and hence appears to call for an overall response. In *general,* how do young children respond to TV ads? The information that research can provide for this question may come in several steps. A first step might be reviewing existing studies to estimate an overall average outcome. Such a review would have results with the form "On average, research indicates a positive (or negative, or neutral) impact of ads on young children."

Notice that such a finding is indeed only a first step. For many questions, policymakers will have questions that go well beyond this. For example, the FTC rules suggested that children under age eight are at unusual risk. Examining this requires looking at different age groups separately. The question then becomes one about an "interaction." Are TV ads especially harmful or deceptive for children of a *particular* age group?

We believe this example illustrates a general rule. In many policy areas, an on-the-average finding will be useful. Yet it is just the first step. What at first appear to be simple "on average" questions often have components that demand further probing. Frequently there is a quick transition to more detailed questions requiring comparisons between subgroups or a search for unusual outcomes. Lesser (1974) says it well in connection with evaluating educational television:

The simple notion "Does it [an educational program] work?" is a tempting one to ask because of its decisive, unhedging sound, but is inadequate because it implies a simplistic search for the single best program for all children. A more rational approach would be to explore the idea of creating different educational programs to look at program effects on different children and under different conditions. For whom does Sesame Street work and for whom does it fail? Under what conditions is Sesame Street effective or ineffective? Summative evaluations must go beyond assessing simple overall effects on children ("Does it work?") and attempt also to answer these more meaningful questions ("For whom and under what conditions does it work?") (p. 144).

*Research needs.* Overall on-average summaries are valuable in basic research as well as in policy analysis. For example, Hall (1978) analyzed many studies of sex differences in decoding nonverbal information. She found that, on average, women are better decoders than men. In basic research, an on-the-average finding is particularly informative when there is little variation in study findings. When studies agree, an average is a good representation of reality. But is an average useful when studies disagree?

One virtue of an average is that tentatively accepting a general if imperfect rule can inform new research. For example, Hall's systematic review with its dozens of studies shows overall sex differences. It would be a mistake to overlook this variable in future research on nonverbal decoding.

On the other side, a danger of an overall summary lies in the "clout" combining dozens of studies can create. It would be a shame if researchers assumed that the question of sex differences in nonverbal decoding has been answered and that the issue is closed. There is variability in the magnitude and even the direction of the differences. Hall explored possible causes for these disparate outcomes. Much remains to be learned about sex differences, and many more data points are needed to complete the picture. Hall's work, including her on-the-average finding, has created a broad background, a context for examining future results.

Basing a "go/no go" decision about future research solely on an average from existing studies can do science a disservice. Future methodological refinements may change the picture dramatically. An example is the controversy over the effects of glutamic acid on IQ. Researchers in the 1940s and early 1950s found that this drug improved the IQ scores of retarded persons. Other research, with better controls, found that the special attention received by people getting glutamic acid, rather than the drug itself, was responsible for the IQ increases (Astin and Ross, 1960). Terminating research when early studies demonstrated glutamic acid's on-the-average effectiveness would have led to incorrect conclusions about a drug given to thousands of people.

Finally, reviews are sometimes initiated to help select new directions for research. Under current economic constraints, hard decisions must be made about which future initiatives look most productive. Averages may provide some guidance. But scientists should insist that, where possible, research summaries provide a fuller representation of reality. For this reason, on-the-average reviews should be routinely supplemented with analyses that look at variability in findings. At a minimum, such analyses will help readers to know if an on-the-average summary is appropriate.

### Where and With Whom Is a Treatment Particularly Effective or Ineffective?

Statisticians distinguish between "main effects" and "interactions." A main effect analysis compares people receiving a treatment to similar people not getting it. An interaction analysis examines whether particular combinations of treatments and recipients work especially well or poorly.

Questions focusing on interactions abound in policy debates. Are TV advertisements harmful for particular age groups, even if they do not harm most children? Are some people more likely to benefit from mid-career job training than others? Are certain sorts of people especially receptive to preoperative surgical information intended to reduce postoperative hospital stays? Research in some fields has already turned up critical interactions. For example, it is difficult to choose among various preschool curricula for children in an "on the average" sense. Yet strong evidence is emerging that children from poor families or with low test scores benefit most from highly structured curricula, while for richer or higher-achieving children curriculum structure hardly matters (Bissell, 1970). An example of a review that deals with interactions appears in Box 2.2.

Single studies often examine interactions. For example, suppose a daycare researcher believes that small groups are particularly valuable for poor children while group size does not matter for richer children. A research design that "crosses" different group sizes with type of child can test this hypothesis.

What if no single study systematically builds in all the interesting combinations of $T$ and $X$ that a reviewer wants to examine? Then the studies *as a group* may offer such information. In the daycare example, perhaps at least one study looked at large groups with rich children, another at large groups with poor children, a third at small groups with rich children, and a fourth at small groups with poor children. Taken together, these four studies give the reviewer some information about whether or not a two-by-two interaction exists. Of course a responsible reviewer must ask about other background features of the four studies. Are the studies fundamentally comparable? Perhaps one took place in an elegant university daycare center while another's home base was a poor public multiservice facility. Then the four small studies are not a good proxy for a single large one that would systematically vary group size and type of child while holding everything else constant. But the point is that collections of studies can shed light on complex interaction questions in a way few single studies can.

A review may find several replications of a particular combination of $X$ and $T$. For example, suppose each of five daycare studies examines the effects of large versus small groups on the development of poor children. Then a reviewer can estimate roughly the consistency, or reliability, of a finding. If

---

**BOX 2.2. A REVIEW THAT ASKED ''WHERE DOES IT WORK AND WITH WHOM?''**

In 1981 Representative Augustus Hawkins, Democrat of California, in his capacity as Chairman of the House Committee on Education and Labor, Subcommittee on Employment Opportunities, asked the General Accounting Office to synthesize what was known about the effectiveness of Comprehensive Employment and Training Act (CETA) programs:

> The Subcommittee is interested in obtaining an assessment of existing evaluation information for at least four types of CETA services—classroom training, on-the-job training, work experience, and public service employment. It would be most helpful if this work were based on a technical review of evaluation designs and products such that it presents and integrates the results of the soundest and most comprehensive CETA evaluations.

Given this request, the General Accounting Office staff did not believe an on-the-average answer would be adequate. So they posed the question, ''For different participants, and for different types of CETA experiences, what are the CETA outcomes?'' This is analogous to our ''Where and with whom does the program work?'' Their results are organized to answer exactly this question. They make clear the problems of using an overall value-added for all CETA participants.

> The effects of CETA varied considerably according to participant characteristics and the type of service they engaged in. Overall, both white and minority women realized statistically significant earnings gains ranging from $500 to $600. Earnings gains for men at $200 were small and not statistically significant . . .
>
> When considered by service type, the picture is more complex. Females profited from classroom and on-the-job training and public service employment, with large gains relative to comparison groups of $1,200 for minority women in on-the-job training and $950 for white women in public service employment. Additionally, minority women in multiple services realized a gain of $1,400. They were the only group to show a statistically significant gain from participation in multiple services. Meanwhile, white men profited from classroom and on-the-job training. Their largest gain was in on-the-job training, at $750; in classroom training, their gain was $400. Minority men realized statistically significant gains only in on-the-job training, but the net impact was large, at $1,150. Intermediate and mixed earners realized statistically significant gains only for on-the-job training. High earners actually appeared

to lose ground by participating in work experience. The high earners, the group with the most discouraging results, represented only 15 percent of the fiscal 1976 participant sample, however, while the group with the best results, the low earners, constituted some 50 percent of the sample (U.S. General Accounting Office, 1982a, pp. 84–86).

---

the five studies have similar outcomes, the reviewer's confidence in the overall finding increases. (Box 2.3 gives a concrete example of programs having different effects in different places.)

### Will It Work Here? What Are Practical Guidelines for Implementing a Treatment in a Particular Setting?

To be relevant to policy, information must be *usable*. Yet a common complaint of local administrators is that research too easily becomes detached from the nitty-gritty details of ongoing programs. Reviews that look at a group of studies, some perhaps several years old, are even further removed. What can a local program manager learn from such efforts?

Too often the answer is "not much." This is because the questions reviewers pose are overly broad. Dilemmas faced by program managers, or school administrators, or doctors, or hospital directors, or even parents, are much more specific. "What drug should I prescribe?" "What curriculum will work best in my school?", "Will day care pose a threat to my child's welfare?" An average from several empirical studies may provide some help and background information. But the individual will still ask, will it work *here,* or will it work for *me?*

The usual scholarly treatise will not answer such questions. They require more personal and situation-specific efforts. For example, some research indicates that financial returns to a college education are far less than most people imagine (Freeman, 1971; Jencks, 1972). What might a high school guidance counselor think, reading a review of these studies? A reasonable conclusion is that, overall, there is little financial gain from going to college. Now suppose a student asks the counselor for advice. The counselor will probably approach the decision in a much more personal way. He will consider the student's particular background, motivation, and interests. He will consider alternative possibilities. Ulti-

---

**BOX 2.3.   ONE PROGRAM EFFECT OR SEVERAL?**

Some interventions may not have the same effect everywhere. An illustration comes from a report from the National Academy of Sciences (NAS). When a review of rehabilitation programs for criminal offenders (Lipton, Martinson, and Wilks, 1975) found very few success stories, the NAS convened a panel to evaluate the evidence. Overall, the panel shared the reviewers' conclusion, but they also stressed some limitations:

> Another limitation on Martinson's gloomy conclusion is that there are some suggestions in recent research reports that interventions involving work and financial support may have a modest impact on postrelease criminal activity. The work-release Program in North Carolina appears to reduce the seriousness, although not the amount, of postrelease criminal activity (Witte 1977). Two California programs have also reported some effect of work release in reducing criminal activity (Jeffrey and Woolpert 1974; Rudoff and Esselstyn 1973), although programs in Massachusetts (LeClair 1973) and Florida (Waldo and Chiricos 1977) have not. Reasons for the inconsistent results are not known; they may relate to specific details of the programs or to local employment conditions, among other things. (Sechrest, White, and Brown, 1979, p. 32).

As the NAS report suggests, similar programs may be differentially effective because of different local conditions. A reviewer of a group of such studies must be careful to avoid casually attributing such differences to normal chance variation in outcomes. Differences in settings or contexts (such as local employment conditions) can lead to major and predictable differences in program success.

mately he will advise this student using far more specific criteria than simply reciting the conclusion of the research review that "on the average a college education offers little economic value-added." Similarly, a doctor prescribing a treatment will use personal knowledge of what idiosyncratic situations his patient faces. We stress here that neither the counselor nor the doctor should *put aside* broad research findings. On the contrary, broad findings should play an important role in any final recommendation. Our point is that they will not play the *only* role.

It is helpful to know from the outset that a review will be used to inform a local decision. This knowledge will lead a reviewer to keep an eye out for the few studies that bear particularly on the local circumstances. It also should focus special attention on case studies or narratives that "personalize" findings. Even if a reviewer is not targeting the effort to a particular setting, including this information can dramatically increase the usefulness of findings at the local level.

Research on the effectiveness of bilingual education programs illustrates this. Many studies have examined special instruction for people whose primary language is not English. One specific format for such instruction is called "transitional bilingual education." In it, children are taught in both their native language and English until they become proficient in English.

A recent review (Baker and de Kanter, 1982) looked at several dozen studies and reached two major conclusions: first, the case for any *particular* bilingual program is not strong enough to justify a legal mandate; second, several effective alternatives to transitional bilingual education exist. These conclusions carry real policy implications:

Since several States have followed the Federal lead in developing programs for language-minority children—in some cases, even legislating transitional bilingual education—our analysis has implications beyond the Federal level . . . There is no reason to assume a priori that an approach that works in a rural Southwest Texas district with a large proportion of second generation Hispanic children should also be applied to a school with a small group of Lao refugees in a Northern city. But Federal policy has been based on such an assumption over the years. A fundamental change in Federal policy is needed (p. 21).

If valid, this broad conclusion is fascinating. And it might be valuable for federal decisionmaking. But it is far less informative for program administrators in particular locales. The school principal in a Texas city with many Spanish-speaking children needs to know which program is likely to work best there. The situation is complex, so clear-cut and unequivocal answers may not exist. Yet a review focusing on setting-by-treatment interactions could help a lot. Are positive results of transitional bilingual education more common for Spanish than for other languages? Does teacher-student ratio influence program effectiveness? Have there been reports of difficulties in implementing a bilingual program that the Texas principal should know about?

These questions require going beyond such conclusions as "we know transitional bilingual education works in some places and fails in others, but we do not know why and cannot, therefore, specify in what situations transitional bilingual education should or should not be used" (p. 24). A review intended to guide implementation would do well to use procedures for examining variation (see Chapter 3) combined with systematic case studies (see Chapter 4).

## Issue 2: Exploring Outcomes versus Testing a Hypothesis

When beginning a research review, an investigator should decide, and make clear to readers, whether the effort is designed to *test* a specific hypothesis or rather to *explore* available information.

If there are guiding hypotheses, they should be specified early on. They can influence the selection of individual studies and the choice of background variables to examine systematically. They can be helpful by suggesting whether the review should aggregate over $X$ (participant type) while comparing different $T$'s (treatments), or aggregate over $T$ while looking at different $X$'s, or let both $X$ and $T$ vary.

*Example:* If the hypothesis is that a soon-to-be-marketed drug has unpleasant side effects, the reviewer should identify studies of that specific $T$ which include as wide a range as possible of $X$. The broader the set of patient circumstances, the more informative the hypothesis test will be. It is important to know if the drug is harmful to even a few people.

*Example:* The hypothesis that a highly structured curriculum is more effective than other curricula for four-year-old children with low IQ test scores would point to studies comparing different $T$'s across a homogeneous group of $X$'s.

*Example:* The hypothesis that drug A works better for young people than for old, while drug B works better for older people than for young, suggests an interaction. Here the reviewer should include studies comparing different $T$'s across different $X$'s. This will allow a comparison of the relative effect of each drug on different types of recipients.

Suppose a reviewer does not begin with a specific hypothesis. The goal may be to tackle an area of research "to see what is known." Then a productive reviewing strategy is to cast as wide a net as possible when searching for studies to include. Including diverse studies increases the chance of turning up provocative findings or relationships. This exploratory work will suggest new directions for systematic future studies.

Hypothesis-testing reviews and exploratory reviews have different emphases. A hypothesis asserts which treatment is most effective; a review then examines empirical evidence to test the hypothesis. Inferences from exploratory reviews flow in the opposite direction—from outcome to treatment. A reviewer might collect thirty studies of nursing home procedures for elderly patients. After identifying those nursing homes with the most positive findings, she reasons backward to speculate as to what procedures followed in the nursing homes might be responsible.

A word of caution. Drawing statistical inferences about relationships uncovered from exploratory analyses is very risky. In the usual "data-snooping" venture, many relationships among variables are examined. In these multiple tests a few statistically significant findings may occur simply through chance. (Hunter, Schmidt, and Jackson (1982) describe this problem in detail and give examples. We discuss the point further in the following section.) Making the effort to define *in advance* the key hypotheses motivating a review will pay off by making statistical analyses more powerful and interpretable.

We do not recommend that a reviewer *invent* hypotheses for this purpose. But discussion sections in original articles, and published comments on the articles, often are rich with speculations about why the results turned out as they did. Hypotheses derived from these speculations can provide a useful organizational framework. For example, a landmark study by Rosenthal and Jacobson (1968) demonstrated that teachers' expectations influence pupils' scores on IQ tests. Many published criticisms of the original study and attempts to replicate it followed. Raudenbush (1983) organized his review of this research around several hypotheses generated from a careful reading of the literature. For example, he systematically examined the suggestion made by critics that studies showing IQ increases offered selective test coaching to experimental children. He found little support for the impact of such coaching.

## Is a Review Overcapitalizing on Chance?

When a reviewer has no formal hypotheses, the task is to explore various findings and insights that emerge from a group of studies. In such reviews there is a particular red flag to remember. Simply searching among many studies for variables significantly related to an outcome can lead to *false positives*. A false positive in this instance is a statistically significant relationship that in fact is a chance occurrence. This idea is no different from the well-known statistical caveat that if a single study examines dozens of separate relationships, each at the .05 level of significance, it is not surprising to see one in twenty of those relationships turn up significant, even though that finding is spurious.

Exploratory data analysis, in a research review just as in a single study, requires an investigator to pay a "penalty for peeking," as Frederick Mosteller once described it. The "penalty" is adopting stricter criteria for statistical significance.

A concrete example can illustrate this. Suppose twenty factors suspected of influencing a trainee's performance on the job are assessed in a single multivariate study. We can rank order the twenty effects from largest to smallest. If we then simply compare the largest to the smallest using a simple, unadjusted $t$-test, there is a good chance they will be significantly different. This can happen even if their true, underlying population effects are identical. The reasons for this misleading finding are sampling error and the intentional selection of extremes. Any simple comparison between the largest and smallest of a group of means must take into account that the two being compared are not chosen at random. Nor are they chosen based on a prior hypothesis. Rather they are being compared simply because in a particular sample they happened to be, empirically, the largest and smallest. Reviewers examining many studies and looking at many statistical comparisons in an exploratory way must guard against this overcapitalizing on chance.

Two suggestions are helpful here. First, a reviewer can pay the "penalty for peeking" by using multivariate statistics that formally incorporate the total number of comparisons being explored. Ideally, however, any significant findings that turn up should still be confirmed with new studies. Second, a reviewer without hypotheses may choose to forgo inferential statistical tests altogether. *Descriptive* indices, such as means and correlation coefficients, can be used instead. Since statistical inference is more rigorous when based on hypotheses, it may be preferable simply to describe the research terrain and to hold statistical tests for future verification of interesting findings.

## Should a Review Divide Studies into Subsets?

The limitations of using statistical significance testing with exploratory reviews are substantial. Many relationships are examined simultaneously. It is therefore inappropriate first to *discover* what seems to be a particularly interesting relationship between variables in a data set, and then to use exactly the same data set to formally *test* its statistical significance. This is overcapitalizing on chance in the extreme.

One constructive alternative is to divide the full collection of studies into two groups. One group is used to explore relationships among variables. This group can generate hypotheses about which treatment components are most effective or which people are helped most. These hypotheses are then tested in a more rigorous statistical fashion using the second group of studies. (For a policy example, see Box 2.4.)

---

### BOX 2.4.  DIVIDING STUDIES INTO SUBSETS: A POLICY EXAMPLE

Klitgaard, Dadabhoy, and Litkhouhi (1981) used exploratory data analysis to answer a question posed by a Pakistani Minister of Education: "Which school policy variables are most effective in improving examination scores?" The authors had no a priori theoretical model to guide their analyses. They decided to reduce the possibility of spurious findings by randomly dividing their sample of 208 Karachi secondary schools into two groups: "Half the data is locked in a safe and not examined. The other half is examined extensively, in an effort to find a 'best regression equation.' The best equation is posited as a model, and then it is tested on the safeguarded half" (p. 102).

This procedure avoided the pitfalls of overcapitalizing on chance. Exploratory analysis of the first subset identified one statistically significant policy variable: teachers' average salary. However, when tested on the second half, the salary variable no longer approached significance. The authors concluded that "the effect 'discovered' in our detailed explorations with the first half of the data set may simply have been an artifact of random fluctuation" (p. 108). Validating findings on the second data set helped to avoid a spurious conclusion.

---

There has been serious investigation (e.g., Francis, 1967) as to what the optimal split is for any set of data, where part of the data will be used to generate hypotheses and the other part to test these hypotheses formally. Mosteller and Wallace (1966) provide an intriguing example. They investigated the disputed authorship, Madison versus Hamilton, of some of the Federalist Papers. They began by dividing into two parts a data set taken from the Federalist Papers where authorship was known. One part generated those words that best discriminated between the two authors. The second part was used to test these findings—to see how the discriminating words held up. Mosteller and Wallace found some "regression to the mean." Some words that discriminated particularly well in the first half turned out to be less good discriminators in the second half. Estimating the size of this regression effect was useful for ultimately assigning authorship of the remaining disputed Federalist papers.

This sort of procedure is valuable in doing a research review. A fraction of the studies can generate hypotheses about effective treatment versions or predictors of program success. The other fraction can then formally assess these hypotheses. The one caveat for breaking the data into parts is that if the entire data set has some systematic bias, this procedure will not eliminate it. Regardless of the format of the analysis, inferences are only as valid as the studies on which the review is based.

## Issue 3: Selecting Studies

Critics of research reviews frequently focus on how studies were originally selected for inclusion. If each of several reviews of rehabilitation programs for prisoners uses a different set of studies, it will not be surprising if they reach different conclusions. Similarly, when reviewers choose a few favorite studies and exclude all others because they are "imperfect," conflicts are no surprise.

We have no single "correct" strategy to suggest here. (Our

discussion of which studies to include focuses on conceptual issues. For a treatment of how to locate studies, see Glass et al., 1981, chapter 3.) Which studies to include depends upon the availability of research reports, how many there are altogether, whether many are published, the frequency and quality of different research designs, and of course the question a reviewer is asking (Light, 1980). Our main suggestion is that each review should clearly specify two things: First, what are the criteria for choosing studies? Second, what are the implications of a particular selection strategy? This recommendation may seem simple, almost trivial. Yet readers familiar with existing research reviews know how rarely this information is provided.

### Option 1: Use Every Available Study

The simplest option conceptually is to include every available study: published and unpublished academic research studies, masters and doctoral theses, and contract research reports available from organizations like the Rand Corporation, SRI, Abt Associates, the Urban Institute, and the National Academy of Sciences. This option avoids the dilemma of choosing among studies and justifying why only some are included. It eliminates debates about which studies are worthy of inclusion.

Including all available studies also has scientific merit. When a reviewer has no a priori hypothesis and wants to explore broadly "what is known" in a research domain, including many diverse data points can help. Scientific precision is less important than identifying interesting trends, patterns, or outliers. Including a wide variety of research designs and treatment variations can enhance this effort.

But a reviewer faces difficult tradeoffs in any plan to track down and include everything. First, if it is clear that a particular study is fundamentally flawed, with obvious statistical errors, we find it hard to argue for its inclusion. We do not believe that wrong information is better than no information.

When studies are excluded, the reviewer should state why, and discuss how the omissions might influence overall conclusions.

Second, some studies are difficult to locate. This is a practical consideration that some people may not find especially compelling. But if a serious search turns up 43 out of 50 existing studies, there is a real question about how much additional time and money can be spent locating the other seven.

Third, substantive differences will eliminate some studies. For example, a treatment or program may be known to change over time. Including very old studies that do not portray the program in its current form, when the question underlying a review is how well the program *currently* works, is foolish. Another example is reviews that compare treatment groups to control groups. Different studies may use different control groups. In the daycare literature, for instance, daycare is usually compared to some alternative. One such alternative, or control group, is raising children at home by a parent. A second is nursery schools. A third is baby-sitters. A reviewer must decide on an appropriate comparison group. This decision can limit the number of included studies.

## Option 2: Stratify by Study Characteristics

An alternative to including every potentially interesting study is to specify a few key categories of studies that must be represented. The first step is to divide all available studies into categories. Then, some studies from each category are selected for the review. This stratification guarantees representation for each important type of study, without forcing every single study into the review. The reviewer analyzes in detail only the modest number of selected studies.

Stratified sampling is especially valuable when study characteristics are systematically related to program outcomes. If one expects that the performance of a preschool program depends upon staff-to-child ratio, or geographic location, it makes sense to ensure that different ratios or locales are in-

TABLE 2.1. RATINGS OF THERAPEUTIC TRIALS OF PORTACAVAL SHUNT
OPERATIONS, 95 INVESTIGATIONS.

| Controls | Degree of enthusiasm | | | Totals |
|---|---|---|---|---|
| | Marked | Moderate | None | |
| Adequate | 0 | 3 | 4 | 7 |
| Poor | 18 | 2 | 1 | 21 |
| None | 50 | 14 | 3 | 67 |
| Totals | 68 | 19 | 8 | 95 |

Source: Chalmers (1982).

cluded in the review. This suggests grouping studies into, say, urban versus rural locations, and then selecting some studies from each group.

Stratified sampling has many benefits. For example, study characteristics such as experimental design are often strong predictors of research outcomes. In a review of 95 studies of portacaval shunt surgery, Chalmers (1982) found a clear relation between how well controlled a research design was and how successful the investigators rated the surgical outcomes. The higher the degree of control, the less enthusiastic the investigators were about the surgery's effectiveness. These findings appear in Table 2.1.

We cannot state precisely how often research design is related to outcomes (see discussion in Chapter 5). But the possibility of its happening illustrates the importance of including studies with different characteristics when feasible. If a reviewer faces an enormous number of studies and is unable or unwilling to include all of them, a stratified sample is often a sensible compromise.

### Option 3: Use Only Published Studies

A third strategy is to include only published studies. They are easier to find. Unlike dissertations and conference papers, they are located in libraries and accessible to all. So omitting unpublished reports saves time and money.

Restricting a review to published studies may also enhance quality control. Most refereed journals have reasonably strict requirements for publication. Studies must undergo careful peer review. This process usually leads to a better technical product.

But including only published documents has a severe drawback that outweighs the advantages. Rosenthal (1978), Glass et al. (1981), and others have written about *publication bias*. Statistically significant findings are more likely to be submitted to a refereed journal, and more likely to be accepted, than nonsignificant findings (Greenwald, 1975). Knowing this, many authors file away their nonsignificant findings and try again. It follows that reviews including only published sources can seriously overestimate treatment effects. An analysis by Smith (1980) bears this out. She presents the results of ten reviews comparing journal articles to other sources. All ten demonstrate a larger average treatment effect for journal articles, sometimes much larger. (For a closer look at publication bias, see Box 2.5.)

---

**BOX 2.5.   IS THERE REALLY PUBLICATION BIAS?**

Scientists have speculated that research findings not reaching statistical significance are less likely to be submitted for publication in refereed journals. And even if they are submitted they are less likely, all other things equal, to be accepted for publication. This has been called "the file drawer problem" (Rosenthal, 1978). For every published research study there may be several sitting in a researcher's file drawer, unsubmitted or unpublished because they did not turn up statistically significant findings.

Greenwald (1975) conducted a survey to pin down actual publication practices. He surveyed both authors and reviewers of articles submitted to the *Journal of Personality and Social Psychology* during a three-month period in 1973. Questionnaires were sent to 48 authors and 47 reviewers; 36 authors (75 percent) and 39 reviewers (81 percent) responded. While the results include only one journal at one time, they nonetheless put a bit of meat on the speculative bones of publication bias. The questions and a summary of Greenwald's results appear in Table A.

TABLE A.   RESULTS OF SURVEY OF *JPSP* AUTHORS AND REVIEWERS TO DE-
TERMINE PREJUDICE TOWARD OR AGAINST THE NULL HYPOTHESIS.

| Question | Mean responses for | | |
| --- | --- | --- | --- |
| | Reviewers | Authors | All |
| 1. What is the probability that your typical prediction will be for a rejection (rather than an acceptance) of a null hypothesis? | .790(39) | .829(35) | .803(74) |
| 2. Indicate the level of alpha you typically regard as a satisfactory basis for rejecting the null hypothesis. | .043(39) | .049(35) | .046(74) |
| 3. Indicate the level of beta you would regard as a satisfactory basis for accepting the null hypothesis. | .292(18) | .258(19) | .274(37) |
| 4. After an initial full-scale test of the focal hypothesis that allows rejection of the null hypothesis, what is the probability that you will | | | |
| (a) submit the results for publication before further data collection, | .408(38) | .588(35) | .494(73) |
| (b) conduct an exact replication before deciding whether to submit for publication, | .078(38) | .069(35) | .074(73) |
| (c) conduct a modified replication before deciding whether to submit, | .437(38) | .289(35) | .366(73) |
| (d) give up the problem. | .077(38) | .053(35) | .066(73) |
| Total | 1.000 | 1.000 | 1.000 |
| 5. After an initial full-scale test of the focal hypothesis that does not allow rejection of the null hypothesis, what is the probability that you will | | | |
| (a) submit the results for publication before further data collection, | .053(37) | .064(35) | .059(73) |
| (b) conduct an exact replication before deciding whether to submit for publication, | .107(37) | .098(36) | .102(73) |

| | | | |
|---|---|---|---|
| (c) conduct a modified replication before deciding whether to submit, | .592(37) | .524(36) | .558(73) |
| (d) give up the problem. | .248(37) | .314(36) | .280(73) |
| Total | 1.000 | 1.000 | 1.000 |

Source: Adapted from Greenwald (1975).
Note: Table entries are means of respondents' estimates of probabilities, based on the number of responses given in parentheses.

What are highlights of these findings? One is that researchers carrying out a study generally predict that their data will lead them to reject their null hypothesis. This is true 80 percent of the time. A second is that if a study leads to rejecting the null hypothesis of no treatment effect or no relationship between variables, researchers are *more than eight times as likely* to submit their results immediately for journal publication than if they cannot reject. A third is that if the findings from the first test of a hypothesis do not allow rejection of the null hypothesis, the average researcher is *more than four times as likely* to simply give up on the problem than if the first findings allow the null hypothesis' rejection.

The survey findings offer one perspective. Evidence from actual published research reviews offers another. If publication bias really exists, then a research review that exhaustively gathers studies from various sources—journals, books, unpublished reports and theses—should find that unpublished studies have less dramatic findings than published ones. White (1982) carried out an extraordinarily detailed review of the relationship between socioeconomic status and academic achievement. He reports the average correlations ($r$) for different types of studies: books, .508; journals, .343; unpublished, .292. These results confirm, from an empirical base, that larger and more significant results are more likely to be published. We believe that the dilemma of publication bias is a serious one, substantiated by both survey and empirical findings.

---

Because of this bias, focusing only on published studies can lead to serious errors. Efforts to track down theses, conference papers, and government reports usually are well worth trying (see Box 2.6). Including information from these different sources allows an estimate of publication bias and enables a reviewer to adjust any generalizations accordingly. When unpublished sources are omitted, a reviewer is obligated to state the potential bias inherent in the summary.

## BOX 2.6. THE VALUE OF THESES AND DISSERTATIONS

Since publication bias affects what studies appear in journals, access to unpublished work is vital. Academic theses offer several strengths. One is at least a minimum level of methodological rigor. Since universities require several faculty members to read each thesis, there is some formal check on quality. Second, a thesis is far more likely than a summary article to provide detailed numerical information. Journal articles frequently report only simple means, variances, and sample sizes. A thesis usually gives additional facts such as the dropout rate or how many different statistical comparisons were tried overall. Third, simply because far more space is available, a thesis can go into more depth about qualitative features: how the program improved over time; how research problems ultimately were resolved; how the high absentee rate reflects external factors not apparent in any summary statistic. These strengths of university-based theses are another reason why reviewers should make a serious effort to go beyond what is most easily available from published journals in the nearby library.

### Option 4: Use a Panel of Experts

Another way to choose studies is to call upon the expertise of acknowledged specialists in a field. In preparing research reviews for congressional committees, the General Accounting Office has found this polling of experts to be particularly useful. The obvious argument in its favor is the value of capitalizing on an expert's accumulated wisdom. Experts will know more than a relative newcomer about special circumstances, strengths, and drawbacks of certain types of studies. For example, an expert in crime and corrections would know that self-selection often crops up in research on innovative ways to rehabilitate criminals. An expert in education would realize that when a special curriculum is given to some children and withheld from others, the children from whom it is withheld sometimes know about it, and their families talk about it outside of school. As a result, the control group's behavior may change, and it may become contaminated as a basis for comparison. Experts can suggest studies that minimize these difficulties and can point out potential problems in others.

A second argument in favor of outside experts is particularly compelling when reviews are done to inform a policy decision. Experts often know which research reports are considered important by policymakers. Some of these studies may be out of the academic mainstream. If a scholarly review omits without discussion studies that policymakers consider central, the review immediately loses face validity.

How should experts be used? One way is to have a panel of experts initially select all studies. Another is to begin with some other initial criterion, such as a thorough library search, and then ask an outside panel for suggestions of additional studies. Or a scientist may locate studies and carry out the review alone; then the review itself may be reviewed by others. The General Accounting Office has used outside experts frequently to criticize and strengthen research reviews (U.S. General Accounting Office, 1981; 1982a).

A reviewer should keep alert for possible biases in expert judgment. For example, policy experts often pay more attention to "large $n$" studies with modest research designs than to well-designed smaller studies. In education research, for example, the Coleman Report on Equal Educational Opportunity (1966), an enormous survey of more than 600,000 students, was able to transform the way a generation of education researchers and policymakers thought about spending money on schools. This happened even though the research design, a sample survey and not a true experiment, did not permit any formal, causal inferences. Expert input should undergo the same careful evaluation as other data sources. (Table 2.2 summarizes this discussion of the various strategies for deciding which studies to include in a review.)

## Issue 4: Generalizing Results

Virtually all reviews share the goal of generalizing findings to some larger population. Studies of Head Start, job training, or coronary bypass surgery are reviewed to inform decisions

TABLE 2.2.   ADVANTAGES AND DISADVANTAGES OF FOUR STRATEGIES FOR
SELECTING STUDIES.

| Strategy | Advantages | Disadvantages |
|---|---|---|
| Include all studies | Completeness | Time and expense |
| | Eliminates debate about "best" studies | Fundamentally flawed studies weaken findings |
| Stratify by study characteristics | Representativeness without 100% inclusion | Requires detailed knowledge about all studies |
| Include only published studies | Easy access | Publication bias |
| | Quality control | |
| Have experts choose studies | Capitalize on expert wisdom | Expert bias (e.g., preference for large samples or frequently cited studies) |
| | Identify studies highly valued by policymakers | |
| | Identify studies outside of academic mainstream | |

beyond the specific circumstances that a few studies might represent. What are the limits on generalizing to broader settings?

Two factors are critical here: how *studies* were selected for the review, and how *individuals* were selected to participate in each study. When a review includes all available studies, or a good sample of them, we can generalize findings to the population of "study outcomes." For example, when a reviewer draws a careful stratified sample of Head Start evaluations, the findings may be generalized to all Head Start evaluation reports; the population from which the sample came. Since the unit of analysis in a review is the *individual study,* we can generalize findings to the larger population of *studies* reporting Head Start evaluations.

Such inferences can be valuable. It is useful to know what most evaluations of Head Start show. But usually this is not the main point of doing a review. The more crucial question is usually what a program like Head Start does or does not do for *individual children*. So most reviews are undertaken to generalize to the larger population of *program participants*. Whether this is possible depends upon how individuals were selected to participate in individual studies. If individual studies use representative samples of participants, our confidence in generalizing from studies will be high. If, however, unusually poor children or children with extraordinarily enthusiastic parents are overrepresented in individual studies, generalizations to *all* Head Start children are unwarranted. The reviewer has no control over how individuals were originally selected for studies. Yet it is critical to take this factor into account when drawing broad conclusions.

Belsky and Steinberg's recent review of daycare findings (1978) illustrates the point. The authors conducted a thorough literature search; the population of available studies was fairly represented. They found very few negative effects of daycare compared to home care. But they are careful to note that children in high-quality, university-based daycare are far overrepresented in their sample of studies. This caveat is important. It tells readers that generalizing their findings to all children and families currently receiving daycare services, most of which are not in university settings, is hazardous at best. Belsky and Steinberg's work illustrates the value of reporting *both* how studies were gathered for a review and how participants were chosen for individual studies.

Focusing on study averages as the unit of analysis limits generalization from reviews to individuals in another way. A goal of many reviewers is to identify relationships between program characteristics and program success. For example, suppose a reviewer wants to know if number of hours spent in a job-training program predicts later income. One can plot this relationship using study averages. It might happen that studies reporting longer average training times also report lower average incomes. This is the finding *across* studies. Next one can examine the relationship *within* each study. It would be no surprise if the direction were reversed: if within a study, individuals getting more training earned higher salaries. This pattern of findings is portrayed in Figure 2.1.

Here, a relationship derived from study means reverses when applied to individuals. What can explain this apparent conflict? One possibility is that programs providing the most training are based in the poorest neighborhoods with high local unemployment. These candidates need a tremendous amount of training to land even low-paying jobs. Meanwhile, programs with short training experiences are located in more

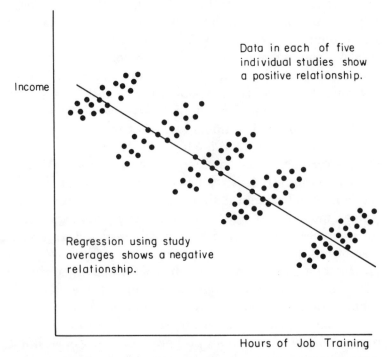

Figure 2.1. Relationship between income and time spent in job training (hypothetical data from five studies).

affluent settings, where higher-paying jobs are more plentiful. *Within each setting,* however, more training is associated with more skills and higher incomes.

Figure 2.1 shows how generalizing a *study-level* analysis directly to individuals can lead to disaster. Job training overall could be judged worthless, when in fact *individuals* in all settings benefited a lot. To avoid such mistakes, always examine both levels of analysis.

### Reviews Can Enhance Generalizability

So far we have focused on hazards of generalizing from study outcomes to individuals. But there is another side to this coin. A research review capitalizing on study-level analyses can provide information that is *not available in any single study.* This information can guide broad implementation of programs. Returning to job training as an example, suppose a small, well-designed program to train paramedics is a resounding success. Twenty trainees *all* find jobs with good salaries and high job satisfaction.

From this one, small, well-done study, one might hope that the positive outcomes will generalize. Suppose, then, the program is implemented widely. With ten times as many trainees, the program meets with unexpected failure. Only a small fraction of new paramedics are employed. An obvious explanation is market saturation—there is employment demand for 20 paramedics but not for 200.

It is hard to fault the evaluator of the small study for having enthusiastic hopes about widespread implementation. There is nothing in the single study's research design or findings that directly suggests the saturation problem. A review of *many* job training studies has a far better chance to identify this issue. Suppose the collection of studies demonstrates mixed success. Some studies show that training works—in others it fails. Such conflicting findings can be exploited for valuable information. Looking *across* the studies, if highly successful programs tend to be small, or are located in areas where employment opportunities abound, whereas failures are large-scale efforts and located where jobs are scarce, the reviewer has identified some key features of program success. The findings from this review tell us when a program is not likely to work, and so they offer systematic guidelines for implementing the programs more widely, and more wisely.

The bottom line, then, is that reviewers cannot afford to rely exclusively on either individual-level or study-level findings. Cross-checking is essential to learn as much as possible about when widespread implementation of a program makes sense.

## Issue 5: Relating Study Characteristics to Outcomes

In the initial stages of organizing a review, it is natural to hope that study outcomes will be orderly, with any conflicts easily explained. But suppose this does not happen, and results conflict? Is that usually bad? Not at all. We believe that conflicting findings offer a particularly rich opportunity for learning about treatment effects. If 100 studies all demonstrate the same positive effect, reporting an overall finding is easy. However, it probably is not very interesting, as the finding will be well known.

How can conflicting study outcomes be reconciled? Sometimes variation among findings can be partitioned into components. First, explainable variation may exist at the level of the *individual participant*. The success of a remedial reading curriculum may depend upon the child's age, the level of parental enthusiasm, and so on. Individual-level effects can be examined within a single study as well as in a review of studies. Second, explainable variation may exist at the *study* level. Children's reading improvement probably is influenced by the type of special reading curriculum, who administers the program, and whether or not the school library has appropriate materials. These *contextual effects* have similar impacts on all participants in any one study, but often vary dramatically across studies.

It is by capitalizing on study-level variation that reviews show their strongest advantage over even the most carefully executed single study (see Box 2.7). One study, with one special program, or research design, or geographical location, cannot examine contextual effects. In contrast, dozens of studies in a review surely will differ in their program characteristics and designs. The challenge is to see which contextual effects can resolve disagreements in findings across studies.

Which attributes of studies are important? While this question depends in part upon the substantive area, there

---

**BOX 2.7. CAPITALIZING ON STUDY-LEVEL VARIATION**

A review can systematically examine an additional source of information that is not available when studies are considered one at a time: variation among studies. Eagly and Carli's (1981) review of sex differences in influenceability provides a fascinating example. The authors examine 148 studies and conclude that men are less influenceable than women, although the overall difference is modest. They pursue this finding further by looking to see if sex of *researcher* is related to study outcomes. Are male scientists more likely to find female influenceability than female scientists? The empirical answer is yes. Eagly and Carli also reanalyze Hall's (1978) review of sex differences in ability to decode nonverbal cues. Hall identified a clear trend of women outperforming men. The reanalysis shows that female authors are somewhat more likely than male authors to find a substantial female advantage. Eagly and Carli conclude: "It appears that at least in these two areas, both male and female researchers portray their own gender more favorably than members of the opposite sex do" (1981, p. 17).

This finding illustrates the benefits of statistically examining study-level variation in outcomes. It is impossible to observe the impact of author's sex on reported results within any single study. The same is true of other study-level variables such as date of publication and type of research design.

is a common core of characteristics most reviews should consider.

## PROGRAM CHARACTERISTICS

Study findings often conflict because similarly labeled programs are actually very different. Just because several research reports describe a program as Head Start, or Job Corps, or Alcoholics Anonymous, one cannot assume the programs implemented in all the studies are really the same. So a first step is to check whether programs with the same name in fact provide the same services. If not, it then becomes possible to refocus attention on the effectiveness of different program versions. For example, daycare programs with small group sizes outperform those with larger groups (Ruopp et al., 1979).

## SETTING CHARACTERISTICS

A program does not operate in a vacuum. It may be more or less effective depending upon who administers it, where it is located, or some other situational factor. Job training is an example. The identical program to train computer programmers may produce different results depending upon where in the United States it is offered. There are more new opportunities for employment in some areas than in others. Success or failure of the same excellent job training can depend upon this geographic fact.

## PARTICIPANT CHARACTERISTICS

A program may turn up more or less effective depending upon who participates in it. These subject-by-treatment interactions are common in human service programs. For example, daycare provides cognitive benefits in a consistent way only to poor children (Belsky and Steinberg, 1978). By overlooking participant characteristics, one can mistakenly conclude that program outcomes are thoroughly unpredictable. Knowing for whom a program works and for whom it fails provides some helpful structure to social planning.

RESEARCH DESIGN

A fourth source of conflicting findings is differing study designs. Table 2.1 illustrated for heart surgery how findings can relate to research design. Research outcomes can be affected by other design characteristics. An example is the *length of time* a treatment is in place (Pillemer and Light, 1979). For instance, there are short-term experiments and longer-term studies investigating effects of TV violence on children's behavior. The short-term studies generally show that seeing violence increases children's aggression, while some longer-term studies show increased aggressiveness in children assigned to a *non*violent TV diet (Leifer, Gordon, and Graves, 1974). Is it surprising that children's reactions depend at least partially upon the length of the treatment? We think not. Short-term changes in people's lives are superimposed upon existing behaviors. Long-term restrictions on children's TV watching are more disruptive: they change normal viewing patterns. Children assigned to nonviolent viewing conditions may well have reacted angrily and even aggressively when forbidden to watch their favorite programs.

A background characteristic related to research design is *date of publication*. As time passes, research refinements are introduced. Scientists may design more reliable outcome measures, or institute other improvements. For example, Hall (1978) reviews studies examining sex differences in decoding nonverbal cues. While women outperform men overall, more recent studies generally show larger sex differences. Hall attributes this to "a combination of more precise measuring instruments and more powerful data analysis" (p. 854). Hall's point is a general one. If variables are measured with error, true relationships between them will tend to be underestimated. Ideally, such underestimates will diminish over time as measuring instruments improve.

ANALYSIS TECHNIQUES

A fifth source of conflict is that different studies often use different strategies for analyzing data. Even if the analyses in each study are done correctly, certain procedures may create artificial but predictable conflicts. For example, the unit of analysis may differ among studies (see Box 2.8). Whether a

---

**BOX 2.8. DIFFERENCES IN THE UNIT OF ANALYSIS CAN EXPLAIN CONFLICTS**

Some research reviews estimate the correlation between two variables. For such reviews, remember that correlation coefficients depend heavily upon the level of aggregation underlying each variable. For example, take educational research where many schools are surveyed, students in each school are tested, and the outcomes are then correlated with certain school characteristics. Two quite different questions easily follow. First, what is the correlation between *individual student* scores and certain school characteristics? Second, what is the correlation between *classroom mean* scores and those same school characteristics? These are related issues. But the precision of the question is important; the first question asks about *dis*aggregated data, while the second asks about aggregated data.

A reviewer might find an enormous range of correlations reported across many studies. A question to ask for each one is whether a reported correlation comes from individual-level data or group-level data. As a general rule, correlations from grouped data are substantially higher than those from individual-level data. In other words, if two analysts examining the same data computed correlations between student scores and school characteristics, and one used individual scores while the second used class means, we would expect the second correlation coefficient to be substantially higher. So a reviewer examining a group of studies using different units of analysis may see correlations that vary greatly.

An example comes from White's (1982) review of studies relating academic achievement to students' socioeconomic status. He divided studies by unit of analysis and found the average correlation to be much larger for aggregated studies (.680) than for studies using the student as the unit of analysis (.245).

statistical analysis is conducted at the individual or group level can dramatically influence an evaluation's findings (Haney, 1974). Singer (1983) has reviewed data from the National Day Care Study (Ruopp et al., 1979). She shows that the strength of relationship between daycare's effects and several policy variables differs when the analysis is done at the classroom level as opposed to the individual-child level. A general rule here is that for any data set where people are more similar within groups than they are across groups, more highly aggregated units of analysis will show a stronger correlation (larger $R^2$). For example, the National Day Care Study consistently found higher $R^2$'s for analyses conducted on data from centers than on data from individual children.

Taking diverse sources of variation formally into account should help a reviewer to sort through a morass of differences among studies. The specific sources presented above can be built into quantitative (see Chapter 3) and qualitative (Chapter 4) reviews. Efforts to resolve conflicting findings can productively begin with this list.

# QUANTITATIVE PROCEDURES

# 3

*"If data analysis is to be well done, much of it must be a matter of judgment, and 'theory,' whether statistical or non-statistical, will have to guide, not command"* (Tukey, 1962, p. 10).

Most recent advances in the reviewing of research are quantitative. There now exists a small arsenal of statistical techniques for producing "on average" statements about collections of research studies. There are also systematic ways to tease out explainable variation in outcomes. After years of reading narrative reviews and asking, "How well does the hard evidence back up the reviewer's claims?," these efforts toward objectivity, efficiency, and statistical precision are appealing.

This chapter on quantitative methods is somewhat different from those in excellent books by Glass, McGaw, and

Smith (1981) and Hunter, Schmidt, and Jackson (1982). The focus here is on how to think about integrating research findings. It is not on deriving various test statistics, or on mathematical details. Rather, we ask questions such as: What are the purposes, advantages, and trade-offs of various techniques? How can we best match choice of technique to a reviewer's purpose? What does a numerical finding "really" tell us? We give special emphasis to visual displays such as graphs and frequency distributions. This reflects our view that a picture is often worth a thousand numbers. A main idea here is examining differences across study findings and working to explain them. We believe that highlighting rather than downplaying conflicts ultimately leads to the biggest payoffs.

## How to Treat Conflicting Findings: Three Views

Some review techniques help to construct on-average summaries rather than zeroing in on why various findings differ. This is similar to emphasizing an average in a single study. Taking an average across a series of outcomes is rarely a difficult conceptual issue. The difficult question is how to treat differences among findings that invariably turn up—the variability of different outcomes around the average. Anyone summarizing 15, or 50, or 100 results with one statistic must face a fact: the cost of using a simple summary index is a loss of information. How one views that fact has important consequences.

### Why Variation Should Never Be Ignored

One option is to emphasize a treatment's average impact without worrying about how outcomes differ. This option is both statistically unsound and substantively unproductive. For decades statisticians have warned about the costs of focusing exclusively on the average performance of people in any one study. When outcomes are distributed in a skewed or multimodal way, or when there are several unusually high or low scores, a data summary should reflect this. A simple average cannot capture such complexity.

Aggregating across many studies is no different. Each study outcome now becomes the unit of analysis. A one-number summary may be convenient, but using it to summarize dozens of outcomes without first determining its suitability is inexcusable.

## Examining Variation as a First Step

Summarizing an entire body of research with a single numerical index leads to sweeping generalizations. Drug A reduces blood pressure by about ten units. A new curriculum cuts the failure rate roughly in half. As we discuss in Chapter 2, producing such sweeping statements is the appropriate goal of some reviews. When a review is undertaken to produce an overall estimate of treatment impact, a key first step is examining the "spread" in study outcomes to see if an average can provide a useful measure. This is conceptually similar to the well-known statistical convention that before comparing treatment and control group means in a single study one should compare the two variances. In either case, ignoring the preliminary step can lead to serious errors.

Examining variation *prior* to producing a summary based on an average can illuminate a critical issue: Do differences in outcomes appear to be only random sampling variation around a *single* population parameter that we want to estimate? Or is there good reason to suspect the existence of a family or *cluster* of distinct underlying population parameters? For example, summarizing the impact of a program such as Head Start with an average requires first determining whether several independent evaluations all appear to assess (with sampling error) the same underlying program, or "effect." The alternative is the existence of several distinct Head

Start programs with different effects on participating children.

## Examining Variation for Substantive Insights

The benefits of examining variation among outcomes go beyond assessing the value of an average. Most reviews report at least some conflicting statistical findings (Jackson, 1980). Rather than viewing such discrepancies as troubling or confusing, we believe they provide an *opportunity* to learn about treatment effectiveness (Light, 1979; Pillemer and Light, 1980a, 1980b). Conflicting outcomes can clarify setting-by-treatment interactions. They can suggest where and with whom particular program types are likely to fail or flourish. Society cannot afford to ignore these substantive insights.

In their relatively brief history, numerical reviews have been criticized for coming up with oversimplified answers. Critics complain that the statistical emphasis leads to reviewers' combining diverse studies in meatgrinder fashion into precise but meaningless single indices. Of course this can happen. But there is nothing about research synthesis that *requires* a reviewer to rely on or produce only a simple overall summary. Some recent and particularly useful reviews also examine, indeed emphasize, variation in outcomes. While this has not been the primary purpose of most reviews, it could and often should be. When a reviewer has no "main effects" hypothesis, but rather is interested in how outcomes differ systematically across different settings and different kinds of people, she may forgo averages altogether and concentrate on more complex analyses.

The specific procedures we present here are useful for both single-answer and multiple-answer reviews. First we describe several statistical indices that reviewers can use for combining findings. Then we present and assess different ways of organizing information for quantitative syntheses. These include constructing distributions and visual displays, assessing the overall impact of a treatment, and statistically examining unusual outcomes or extreme findings.

## Indices of Treatment Impact

Many research reviews are initiated to compare people receiving a treatment with those who are not. How do people receiving a "special" treatment—information about surgery, or job training, or a drug for high blood pressure—compare with people in the "usual" or "control" condition? Of course, studies can become far more complicated than this. For example, sometimes they involve comparing several different treatments to one another. But in many cases the key question boils down to a comparison between two groups. Our discussion will focus on this situation.

Within any single study, each participant will have a measured outcome—income, length of illness, blood pressure. When a reviewer combines the results of many studies, the study rather than the individual participant becomes the unit of analysis. So a first decision is choosing how to measure treatment impact for each study as a whole. For research reviews, the two most common measures are statistical significance and effect size.

### Statistical Significance

Most research about the effectiveness of treatments leans heavily on tests of statistical significance to "decide" an issue. Do differences between treatments and control groups exceed what is expected simply due to sampling error or chance? This emphasis on significance testing carries over quite naturally to research reviews. When treatment and control groups are compared in each of several studies, the $p$-value from each comparison gives one way of interpreting treatment effectiveness. A first cut at aggregating across studies comes from a simple tally of findings. If most studies of a treatment show a statistically significant positive impact, this is a preliminary indication that, in a broad sense, "it works."

## Effect Size

Examining statistical significance across a group of studies is not the only way to aggregate findings. Nor is it usually best. After all, significance tests just give the probability that when a null hypothesis is true, observed differences between treatment and control groups are due to chance. Such tests are heavily influenced by sample sizes. Very small, even trivial, differences in very large samples can turn up statistically significant. More likely a reviewer's main question is whether a difference has practical significance. A new drug to reduce blood pressure may have a statistically significant impact. But suppose the average *magnitude* of the effect is only, say, one point. Then doctors may be reluctant to prescribe it, especially if it is expensive.

Effect sizes provide simple but useful estimates of how valuable a treatment really is. For example, take the common situation of comparing *mean scores* between two groups. Then an estimate of effect size (Glass, McGaw, and Smith, 1981) is simply the difference between the two group means, divided by the control group's standard deviation:

$$ES = \frac{\bar{X}_t - \bar{X}_c}{S_c}$$

To illustrate, suppose that a study compares two groups of teenagers. One group gets special academic tutoring while the other gets just the usual schooling. If after a period of time the average math score for the tutored group is 110, while the average for the control group is 100 with a standard deviation of 20, then the effect of tutoring is $ES = (110 - 100)/20 = .5$, or one-half a standard deviation. Some authors (e.g., Hunter, Schmidt, and Jackson, 1982) suggest using a pooled standard deviation rather than the control group's standard deviation.

But the basic idea is the same. Notice that expressing effect sizes in standard deviation units makes it possible to compare outcomes across different studies. For example, Study A may have an effect size of .2 standard deviation units, while Study B has an effect size twice as large (.4 standard deviation units), and so on. (Box 3.1 discusses the case of studies with no control groups.)

*Proportions* sometimes are more informative than averages. For example, in evaluating the impact of remedial education programs we may be more interested in the proportion of children who are promoted to higher grades than in average test scores. Or the proportion of people who live longer than five years following surgery for cancer may be more interesting than average postoperative longevity. The effect size for proportions is simply $ES = P_t - P_c$, where $P_t$ and $P_c$ are proportions in the treatment and control groups. (Under some circumstances, a transformation may be appropriate;

---

**BOX 3.1.  CAN EFFECT SIZES BE COMPUTED FOR STUDIES WITHOUT CONTROL GROUPS?**

The standard procedure for calculating effect sizes compares a treatment group to a control group. Is an estimate of effect size possible when studies lack controls? Perhaps, depending on the substantive question.

Andrews, Guitar, and Howie (1980) suggest an alternative in their review of treatments to combat stuttering. Since most studies in their review are not comparative and do not have a formal control group, they could not compute effect sizes in the usual way. Instead, pointing out that extensive earlier research had convincingly demonstrated that stutterers rarely improve "on their own, in the absence of treatment," these reviewers argue that pretreatment scores can be used as a proxy for control group performance. They estimate an effect size for each study by comparing the mean after treatment with the pretreatment mean, and dividing by the pretreatment standard deviation. The key to this procedure is clearly the validity of their assumption that stutterers would not improve if left untreated.

---

see Glass, McGaw, and Smith, 1981.) This measure is clearly a simple one: if 80 percent of job trainees are employed compared to 60 percent of untrained controls, the effect of training is .80 − .60 = .20. (A drawback of this simple difference between proportions is difficulty in interpreting nonlinearities. For example, perhaps reducing the school dropout rate from .55 to .50 is not equivalent to reducing it from .10 to .05. Then an alternative measure is $ES = P_t/P_c$.)

Sometimes the key question is about the *distribution* of outcomes across studies. For instance, educators have been interested for years in what happens to weak students if they are tracked rather than placed in regular heterogeneous classrooms. It turns out that initially low-achieving students placed in regular classes show more variation in performance: some improve dramatically, others fail miserably (Franseth and Koury, 1966). When comparing variation between two samples, a simple procedure is to compute a ratio of standard deviations, or $S_t/S_c$. This ratio allows us to describe comparative variability in a simple way, such as the treatment group having "twice" or "one-half" the variability of the control group. When a treatment has no special impact on variation among participants, the expected value of the ratio is one.

Which index of effect size is best? This depends upon the substantive question motivating a review. A caveat here is that if studies do not report essential numerical information, this of course limits the possibilities. For example, standard deviations cannot be compared if they are not available. Glass, McGaw, and Smith (1981) and Rosenthal (1983) present several formulas for estimating effect sizes when the only information available is a test statistic, such as $t$, $F$, or $\chi^2$. Another alternative is trying to get missing information directly from authors.

## Visual Displays

Let us assume that a way of measuring treatment impact has been chosen. Now the real work of quantitative synthesis begins. The best starting point is visual displays. The simplest way to get a general indication of treatment impact is to construct a picture that captures the flow of statistical results. We can suggest several ways to do this.

### Frequency Distributions

When studies all estimate the same underlying population parameter and variation in outcomes is entirely attributable to chance, the central limit theorem tells us that the outcomes of studies with reasonably large sample sizes should be distributed roughly normally around the "true" population value. To illustrate this, we examine an effect-size distribution with various values of $ES = (\bar{X}_t - \bar{X}_c)/S_c$. Such a distribution is easy to produce using computer simulation. Figure 3.1 gives the results of generating 200 randomly selected "studies" from a population with the following characteristics: treatment group mean = 105; control group mean = 100; treatment group standard deviation = 10; control group standard deviation = 10. The population effect size is $(105 - 100)/10 = .5$. Treatment and control group sample sizes are equal for each individual study and were randomly selected from a uniform distribution of $n = 10$ to $n = 100$ across studies.

Figure 3.1 shows that, with 200 studies, most with reasonably large sample sizes, the distribution of effect sizes when comparing two sample means is well behaved and symmetrical. This strongly suggests the existence of a single underlying population difference between the two groups. So when dealing with a large number of studies, such as 200, a reviewer can assume that a random distribution of effect sizes comparing two means behaves well, even when sample sizes vary by a factor of ten across the studies. But when a review has far fewer studies, chance fluctuation should be more pronounced. The distribution with only 20 studies in Figure 3.2 illustrates this. Even with only 20 studies, however, this dis-

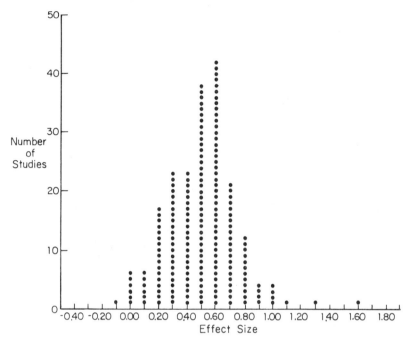

Figure 3.1. Frequency distribution of effect sizes for 200 studies estimating a single population effect (computer simulation).

tribution serves as a first, rough check for extreme skewedness or bimodality.

It is interesting to compare real-world outcome distributions with these ideal forms. Klitgaard, Dadabhoy, and Litkouhi (1979) provide an exotic example using standard deviations as an outcome. They examined variability in standard deviations of science scores across 170 schools in Kara-

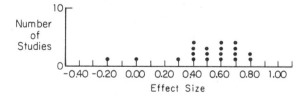

Figure 3.2. Frequency distribution of effect sizes for 20 studies estimating a single population effect (computer simulation).

chi, Pakistan. The distribution is presented in Figure 3.3. It is highly symmetrical, supporting the idea that "much of the variability in standard deviations among schools can be attributed to sampling error" (p. 81).

A second example comes from Kulik and Kulik's (1982) review of the effects of ability grouping on secondary school students' achievement. They identified 51 studies comparing exam performance of students in grouped and ungrouped classes. The outcome measure is effect size. Figure 3.4 shows that the distribution of outcomes is again quite symmetrical. The average effect size of .10 appears to be a reasonably good summary.

This simple graph highlights the value of systematic quantitative summaries. The 51 individual studies vary considera-

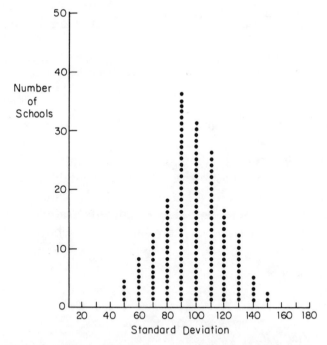

Figure 3.3. Frequency distribution of standard deviations of science scores in 170 Karachi schools (adapted from Klitgaard, Dadabhoy, and Litkouhi, 1979).

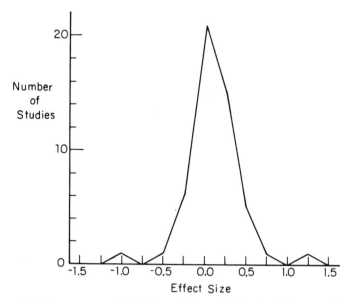

Figure 3.4. Frequency distribution of the effects of ability grouping on student achievement (from Kulik and Kulik, 1982).

bly: 36 favor ability grouping, 14 favor ungrouped classes, and 1 shows no difference. Only 10 comparisons reached statistical significance, and 8 of these favor grouping. Effect-size estimates range from "high positive" to "high negative." Yet when portrayed as a group, the pattern of results is not at all chaotic. Indeed, the distribution of effect sizes is surprisingly orderly around the average value of .10. In general, when the true effect of a treatment is near zero, there will be a mix of positive and negative findings, with only a few scattered significant effects. A simple graphical display can clarify the order in such a pattern.

These simple procedures for constructing distributions are descriptive rather than inferential. They do not provide a definitive "test" of the population distribution. But a graph can present a warning signal when outcomes are clearly incongruent with a one-population-value situation. Figure 3.5 illustrates this, presenting a distribution of effect sizes when the

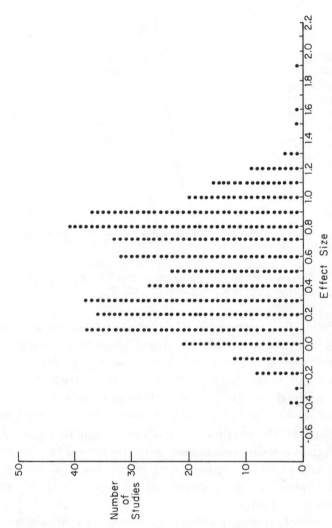

Figure 3.5. Frequency distribution of effect sizes for 400 studies estimating two population effects (computer simulation).

underlying population distribution is *bimodal.* Figure 3.5 was generated using two different treatment group population means: 108 and 102. The control group mean equals 100. All groups have the same standard deviation of 10. Thus the population effect sizes are .8 and .2. The computer randomly generated 200 effect sizes from each population. The distribution of effect sizes in Figure 3.5 has two modes; they are clear from even casual inspection. Using a single overall average to summarize all of these outcomes would miss the bimodality, which possibly is the most interesting feature of the entire picture.

### The Funnel Display

A second graphic approach capitalizes on a well-known statistical principle: as sample size increases, sample statistics come to estimate an underlying population value more and more precisely. In other words, as $n$ increases, variation due to sampling error decreases. At an extreme, if the *entire* population of scores—say all trainees in jobs programs around the country—are included in one study, then the population average can be determined without any sampling error.

*1. Do all studies come from a single population?* This simple relationship between sample size and sampling error helps us to see whether several studies really estimate the same population value, and hence whether a single summary statistic is appropriate. The graphical procedure goes as follows. Plot quantitative outcomes on the horizontal axis. Plot the sample size for each study on the vertical axis. If all studies comes from a single underlying population, this graph should look like a funnel, with the effect sizes homing in on the true underlying value as $n$ increases.

To illustrate the funnel display, we again use computer simulations. Figure 3.6 presents the pattern of effect sizes and sample sizes when each of 200 studies estimates a single underlying population difference between treatment and control group means. The population treatment mean is 110. The control group mean is 105. Both groups have a standard deviation of 10. The population effect size is therefore .5. Sample sizes were chosen randomly from a uniform distribution of 10 to 100. Figure 3.6 indeed looks like a funnel, with less variation among the larger-sample-size findings than among the smaller-sample-size findings. The funnel suggests that the 200 outcomes represent random selections from a single large population. No multiple modes appear in the picture.

Klitgaard, Dadabhoy, and Lithouhi (1979) again provide a real-world example. They plotted standard deviations of science scores in 142 Pakistani schools against sample size (Figure 3.7). Notice the funneling of outcomes with increasing sample size. This led the authors to conclude that the convergence was what "one would expect if in fact all students were samples from a single normal population" (p. 82).

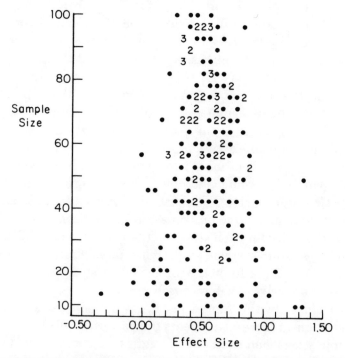

Figure 3.6. Funnel distribution of effect sizes for 200 studies estimating a single population difference between means (computer simulation).

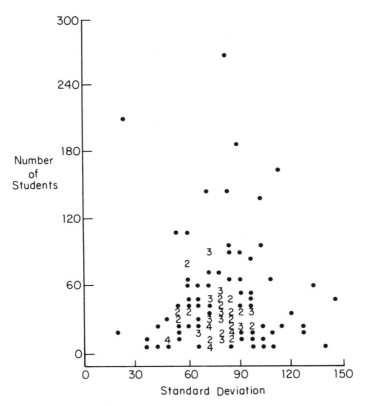

Figure 3.7. Standard deviations of science scores in 142 Karachi schools plotted against sample size (adapted from Klitgaard, Dadabhoy, and Litkouhi, 1979).

*2. Searching for publication bias.* Funnel displays also can help to identify publication bias. It is well documented that studies reporting statistically significant outcomes are more likely to be published and thereby included in research reviews (see discussion in Chapter 2). The systematic omission of well-done studies that fail to reach statistical significance can seriously bias a review. We may overestimate the value of a treatment because only evaluations reporting "successes" are readily available. But for any particular research review, how can we know whether publication bias exists? A good first step is to create a funnel display. The shape of the funnel will at least suggest whether an obvious publication bias exists. Publication bias will modify the shape of the funnel in one of two ways.

First, suppose the true population effect size is zero. Then treatment and control group means are, on the average, identical: yet a few studies will still reach statistical significance due to chance. These will be either (a) studies with very large positive effects or (b) studies with very large negative effects or (c) studies with smaller effects but with very large sample sizes. If publication bias exists, then small-sample studies showing small effects are not likely to appear in journals, since their effect sizes will not be statistically significant. When this happens, the middle of the funnel display will appear "hollow." Figure 3.8 demonstrates this. A computer generated 200 effect sizes with both treatment and control

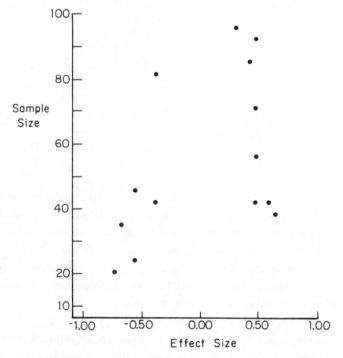

Figure 3.8. Funnel plot when publication bias exists and population effect size is zero (computer simulation).

population means of 100. The standard deviations are 10, and sample sizes are chosen randomly from a uniform distribution spanning 10 to 100. The many outcomes not reaching statistical significance were then eliminated. The hollowness in the center of the funnel display is obvious.

What happens when the true population effect size differs from zero? Then publication bias shows up in a different form. Small-sample studies showing small effects will still be statistically nonsignificant. Therefore they will not appear in the funnel. So there should be a bite out of the funnel where it approaches zero. We simulated this case with a population treatment mean of 105, a control mean of 100, standard deviations of 10, and sample sizes randomly selected from a uniform distribution spanning 10 to 100. Figure 3.9 shows that,

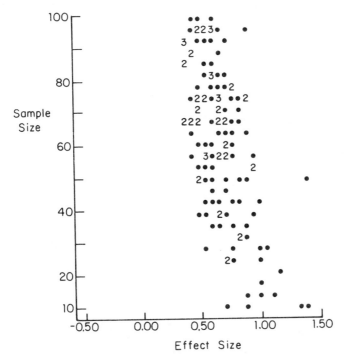

Figure 3.9. Funnel plot when publication bias exists and population effect size is .5 (computer simulation).

because statistically nonsignificant results are omitted, a pronounced bite or chunk is taken out of the display for effects near zero. Notice that the bottom of the funnel informs us about possible publication bias, while the top suggests whether studies are tapping one or a cluster of populations.

Our analysis of data presented in Devine and Cook's (1983) review of educational programs for surgical patients provides a real-world illustration. Figure 3.10 presents effect size plotted against sample size for published studies only. The missing bite from the display for effect sizes near zero is apparent. This should signal a reviewer that publication bias is a strong possibility. If ignored, it can lead to an overestimate of program success. But Devine and Cook's review includes dissertations as well as journal articles, so the issue of possible bias can be examined directly. Figure 3.11 presents the combined funnel when dissertations are included along with published articles. Notice that the bite out of the lower left corner of the

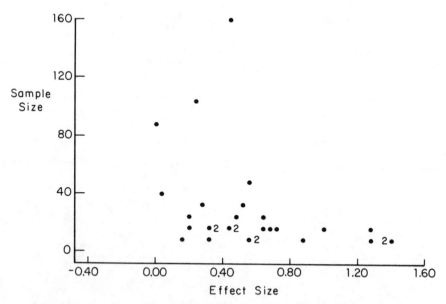

Figure 3.10. Funnel plot for published studies only: analysis of data from Devine and Cook's (1983) review of psychoeducational programs for surgical patients.

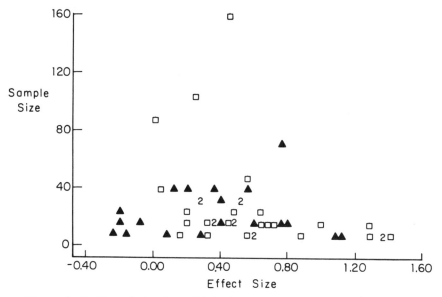

Figure 3.11. Funnel plot for published (□) and unpublished (▲) studies combined: analysis of data from Devine and Cook (1983).

funnel largely disappears. This is due to near-zero and negative effects that appear primarily in dissertations. It also explains Devine and Cook's observation that the average program effect is larger for published studies than for unpublished studies.

*3. Changing population estimates over time.* The funnel display also aids in examining *historical trends* in the precision of scientific estimates. One view of the world is that, as more and more data accumulate under improved experimental conditions, knowledge converges upon underlying truths. For example, as we design stronger and stronger evaluations of Head Start, we are better able to close in on its "true" effect. If this idea is correct, estimates of the effect of a program, or relationship, should have *less variation over time.* On the other hand, suppose programs really work differentially well in different places. Then methodological improvements over time should not narrow the variation among findings. Rather, the main value of improvements would be in making it possible to identify predictable differences in program effectiveness.

Funnel displays can help to move this discussion beyond philosophical debate. Plot estimates of effect size along the horizontal axis and date of publication of a study on the vertical axis. Figure 3.12 demonstrates this procedure for studies taken from Hall's (1978) synthesis of findings about sex differences in decoding nonverbal cues. Hall reports effect sizes from 29 studies of decoding in the visual mode. Women generally outperform men. The average effect size is .32. Publication dates range from 1929 to 1976. Notice that the display does not converge to a single value as time passes. Hall reports that the extent of women's superiority increases over time, which she attributes to "more precise measuring instruments and more powerful data analysis" (p. 854). Our funnel analysis shows that this increased precision does not dramatically reduce *variation* in estimates of effect size.

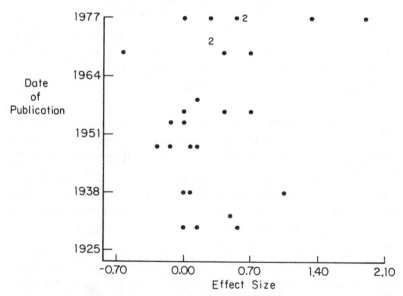

Figure 3.12. Plot of effect size by date of publication: analysis of data from Hall's (1978) review of sex differences in decoding nonverbal cues.

Figure 3.13 presents effect sizes from Devine and Cook's (1983) review of psychoeducational interventions for surgery patients plotted against date of publication. Again, the display does not show convergence over time. The range of parameter estimates actually *increases* over time (the funnel is inverted), although this might simply reflect the greater number of modern studies.

Our belief is that these few examples are telling us something important. The passage of time, with its accompanying improvements in the conduct of social research, sometimes will not lead to converging effect size estimates. (For an example from the natural sciences, see Box 3.2.) Since treatment effects depend upon many situational factors, progress may produce a better and more systematic understanding of

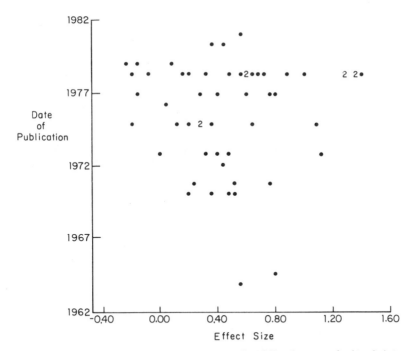

Figure 3.13. Plot of effect size by date of publication: analysis of data from Devine and Cook's (1983) review of psychoeducational interventions for surgery patients.

how outcomes *differ* across settings. In other words, progress may clarify and explain divergence that exists in the world and is correctly captured by a group of research findings.

## Assessing Overall Impact

When a reviewer is interested in a treatment's overall impact, and when graphic displays suggest that an overall summary is

---

**BOX 3.2.   IS SCIENTIFIC PROGRESS ORDERLY? HISTORICAL FUNNELS IN PHYSICS**

Fascinating examples of historical "funnels" come from physical as well as social science. A review of particle properties in physics (Particle Data Group, 1976) examined historical trends directly. The graphs in Figure A give estimated values for the masses of several particles plotted against date of publication. The values and confidence limits were derived by combining several experiments or independent observations. It is interesting to see that while parameter estimates generally become more precise over time, "progress" is not always uniform. Notice also that modern values can fall entirely outside the confidence limits developed around early estimates. These findings contrast with the view that science (especially physical science) always zeros in on "truths" in a predictable and orderly fashion. We quote from the authors of the review:

> We show these figures not only to demonstrate that there is not much change in these averages in the usual case, but also to show that there exist cases with relatively large changes. There is a psychological danger in preparing tables of "right" answers. The old joke about the experimenter who fights the systematics until he or she gets the "right" answer (read "agrees with previous experiments"), and then publishes, contains a germ of truth (presumably, those who compile and average experimental results are also not immune to this disease). A result can disagree with the average of all previous experiments by five standard deviations, and still be right! Hence, perhaps it is of value to show that large changes can (and do) sometimes occur (p. S19).

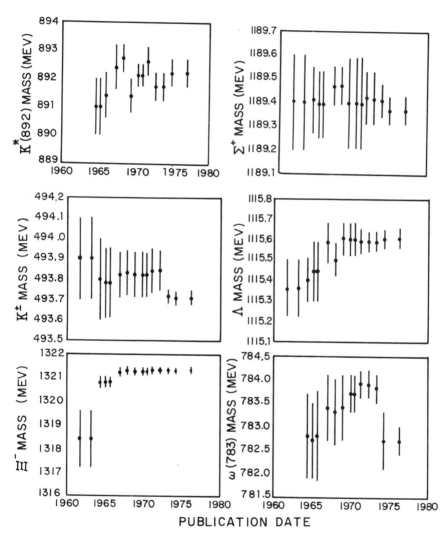

Figure A. Averages of the masses of various particles as a function of date of publication of Review of Particle Properties (from Particle Data Group, 1976).

appropriate, a number of options are worth considering. Several statistical procedures can be called upon, each with benefits and drawbacks. These procedures have been described in detail elsewhere (e.g., Glass, McGaw, and Smith, 1981; Rosenthal, 1978). Here we emphasize when to use each, and point out strengths and weaknesses.

## Taking a Vote

All available studies can be divided into three groups: those with significantly positive, those with significantly negative, and those with nonsignificant outcomes. Add up the number of studies falling into each category. Whichever outcome gets the most votes is declared the winner. Vote counting is quick and easy. It can almost be done on the "back of a napkin."

Vote counting's main attraction is its simplicity. It quickly confirms strong and consistent findings. For example, if a vote count shows nine out of ten studies with strong positive program effects, the evidence for program success is convincing. When the situation is more complex, however, vote counts can lead to serious errors. Light and Smith (1971) discuss a U.S. Office of Education review of the effectiveness of ESEA Title I funds. Of 189 separate evaluations, each conducted at the 0.05 level of significance, 58 showed that Title I significantly improved student performance, 50 showed students losing ground, and 81 showed no significant change in either direction. A vote count would lead to an on-balance conclusion of "no effect," since the modal outcome was "no change," and the significant pluses roughly balance the significant minuses. But concluding that Title I has no effect misses the point. If the program is ineffective, only about 5 percent of the studies should report significant outcomes due to chance alone (using a .05 probability of Type I error). Five percent of 189 studies is fewer than 10 studies. Yet 108 studies actually showed significant outcomes. This very large number of significant effects certainly does not reflect random variation around zero. "Our conclusion from the data . . . is that there are several truths. Title I programs vary in their effects; some help, some hurt, and some make no difference at all" (Light and Smith, 1971, p. 44). So a simple vote count would ignore the pile-up of far more studies than expected in the tails of the outcome distribution.

A second problem of vote counting is that it is not very powerful in a statistical sense. When sample sizes and effect sizes are small, a simple vote count will often fail to identify a significant overall treatment effect. For example, Hedges and Olkin (1980) show that with 20 studies of sample size 30 and a population effect size of .5, a vote count will fail to detect the substantial positive treatment effect 75 percent of the time! This is a serious drawback. In social science, where both sample sizes and effect sizes are frequently small, such low power is unacceptable.

A third drawback is that vote counts, and the significance tests on which they are based, tell us little about the *size* of an effect. "To know that televised instruction beats traditional classroom instruction in 25 of 30 studies—if, in fact, it does—is not to know whether television wins by a nose or in a walkaway" (Glass, McGaw, and Smith, 1981, p. 95). Because statistical significance depends so heavily on sample size, studies with small effects can be highly significant if a sample is large enough. So even if every one of 30 studies in a review reports findings that are statistically significant, a vote count does not tell us whether they are large enough to matter in practice. (Box 3.3 illustrates questions raised by vote counts.)

### Combined Significance Tests

A more elaborate procedure for drawing a single "grand" conclusion from a group of studies is to combine each study's individual significance test into an overall pooled test. Rosenthal (1978) describes nine ways to accomplish this. For example, take the method of adding $Z$ scores (standard nor-

---

## BOX 3.3.  A REVIEW BASED ON VOTE COUNTING

Warr and Perry (1982) examined 38 studies of women's psychological well-being and paid employment status. They identified six indices of women's well-being and defined several categories of women, such as single women, married women, married women with children at home, and so on. They presented a summary of their findings using the vote counting format. A summary of their results for four of the six indices is presented in Table B. This table illustrates that a vote count can summarize findings yet also raise many questions. For example, the vote count gives no information about sample sizes in the various studies. It gives no information about the quality of the studies. It gives no information about the effect size or practical significance of statistically significant findings. Not all reviewers are as careful as Warr and Perry, who specify that these results "should be examined in conjunction with the

TABLE B.  SUMMARY OF STUDIES COMPARING WOMEN'S PSYCHOLOGICAL WELL-BEING AND THEIR PAID EMPLOYMENT STATUS.

| | Indices of psychological well-being | | | | | | | |
| --- | --- | --- | --- | --- | --- | --- | --- | --- |
| | Suicide and attempted suicide | | Diagnosed psychiatric illness | | Psychiatric morbidity | | Psychological distress | |
| Categories of women | + | ns | + | ns | + | ns | + | ns |
| Women in general | 2 | | 2 | 1 | 2 | 3 | 2 | 4 |
| Single women with no children at home | | | | | 2 | | 1 | |
| Single women in general | 1 | | | | 1 | | 1 | |
| Married women with no children at home | | | | | | | 1 | 3 |
| Married women with children at home | | | | | | | 1 | 6 |
| Other groups of women with children | | | | | | | | 3 |
| Married women in general | 1 | | | 2 | | 2 | 1 | 8 |
| All of the above comparisons | 4 | | 2 | 3 | 5 | 5 | 7 | 24 |

*Source:* Adapted from Warr and Perry (1982).

*Note:* + = positive, ns = not significant. Comparisons identified as positive are those in which employed women have significantly higher psychological well-being than those who are unemployed. No cases of a negative association between employment status and psychological well-being were located.

more detailed accounts in the text because it inevitably omits consideration of important additional variables . . . Furthermore, the quality of research in this field is rather uneven, so some studies appearing in [this
table] are less adequate than others; specific design failings have been
noted throughout the text . . ." (p. 510).

---

mal deviates). The $Z$ scores from each individual test are simply added across studies. This sum is divided by the square
root of the number of studies. The probability level associated with this total score gives an overall level of significance for all the studies in a review. Combined significance
tests are computationally simple and generally require knowing only the sample size and the value of a test statistic ($t$, $Z$,
or $F$) or exact probability level for each study.

The main benefit of pooling results from the individual
data sets is the increased *power* of the overall comparison.
The procedures Rosenthal summarizes do this without requiring access to raw data. The larger the overall sample size,
the more likely that a certain underlying effect size will be
detected as statistically significant. Combined significance
tests capitalize on this fact. Grouping studies together creates
a sample size for the overall test that is far larger than in any
one study.

Maximizing power is particularly useful when a program
has a modest but consistent effect. For example, assume program A is more effective than program B, but that the true
difference is small. If A and B are repeatedly compared using
small samples, the finding, on average, should be small differences favoring A. But many of these small differences will not
be statistically significant. A reviewer may therefore conclude
that the effect is not statistically reliable. Combining many
small but consistent findings gives a better chance of correctly detecting the small difference.

Rosenthal (1978) presents a worked example illustrating
this point. Five studies report one-tailed $p$ values of .12, .01,

.72, .07, and .17. The evidence for a reliable statistical effect is not impressive. A vote count, for example, would not turn up a treatment effect, since only one of the five outcomes is significant at the .05 level. But the method of adding $Z$'s across the five studies produces a highly significant overall result. The $Z$ scores for the five studies are 1.17, 2.33, $-.58$, 1.48, and .95. The combined $Z$ score is computed by $\Sigma Z / \sqrt{N}$, or $5.35 / \sqrt{5} = 2.39, p = .009$.

These procedures can be very useful, although they answer a limited question. For example, an overall significance test tells us nothing about the *distribution* of outcomes. Yet this information can be crucial. Suppose a significant overall effect turns up. There might be several explanations. One is that findings are consistently significant across all studies. Another is that only one large study found a significant effect, while several others found essentially nothing. So the one large study dominates the group.

But suppose a significant effect does not turn up. This could be a consistent no-effect finding across all the studies. Or there could be substantial numbers of both positive and negative outcomes that cancel each other out when combined. We therefore recommend that *combined significance tests always be accompanied by the distributional analyses described earlier.*

A second major limitation is connected to publication bias. This bias can create a real problem for overall significance tests, since significant outcomes are overrepresented among the available studies.

Rosenthal (1980) has called this dilemma "the file drawer problem": "The possibility that the journals are filled with the five percent of the studies that show Type 1 errors while the file drawers back at the lab are filled with 95 percent of the studies that show nonsignificant results of $p > .05$" (p. 12). Rosenthal suggests a formula for determining just how many unpublished no-effect studies would have to exist in order to invalidate a significant combined probability based on published studies:

$$X = [ ( \sum_{i=1}^{k} Z_i )^2/2.706] - k.$$

Here $X$ is the fail-safe $N$, the number of file drawer studies necessary to bring the overall $p$ above .05; $k$ is the number of studies in a review; and $\sum_{i=1}^{k} Z$ is the sum of the individual $Z$ scores, across the $k$ studies. If $X$ is a very large number, Rosenthal argues, the file drawer problem should not create drastic worry. For example, in a review of 345 studies he calculated that 65,123 unpublished studies showing no effects would have to be crammed into file drawers to overturn the combined significance of the 345 published studies (Rosenthal and Rubin, 1979).

Computing a fail-safe $N$ is a useful step, although it does not fully solve the problems of publication bias. For example, in a review of 345 studies we would interpret findings differently if there were 50 no-effect findings as opposed to 50,000. Yet both these numbers are less than the 64,345 fail-safe $N$. We know of no easy way to estimate precisely the impact of unpublished research on conclusions drawn from studies in hand.

With all these caveats, how valuable is the technique of combining significance levels in a research review? When only a few studies are available, say five or ten, the increase in power can help to tease out subtle program effects. So the combining may be helpful. With many studies the combined sample size can become so large that even tiny effects will turn up statistically significant: "For most problems of meta-analysis, however, the number of studies will be so large and will encompass so many hundreds of subjects that null hypotheses will be rejected routinely" (Glass, McGaw, and Smith, 1981, p. 99). Here the combined test delivers little new information and does not help a reviewer to assess *practical* significance. This has led some reviewers to deemphasize statistical tests and to focus instead on the magnitude of treatment effects.

## Average Effect Sizes

How can we tell when an effect is large enough to matter in *practical* terms? Some measure of effect size is necessary. Glass (1976, 1977; Glass, McGaw, and Smith, 1981) has written widely on using effect size statistics in reviews. The most common index, *ES,* is defined earlier in this chapter. It is the difference between means of the treatment and control groups divided by the control group standard deviation. Expressing effect sizes in such standardized units makes it possible to compute an average across different studies. An average effect size across studies provides a general measure of treatment impact just as an average score across people in one study is one way of summarizing their various individual performances.

Average effect sizes are becoming a common way to report the value of a treatment. An example is Devine and Cook's (1983) review of whether presurgical interventions can reduce postoperative hospital stays. They found from 34 studies that the average effect size of an intervention is approximately half a standard deviation. On average, people receiving an intervention had half a standard deviation shorter postoperative hospital stays than similar "untreated" people. In concrete terms, the average postoperative stay was shortened by approximately a day and a half, based on the usual average stay of about seven days.

For estimates of effect size to have practical meaning, we need some basis to judge them. How large is large? There is no absolute scale. Effect size averages are most interpretable when compared with other findings that we know something about. Cohen (1977) offers some very general guidelines. Effects of .5 are generally large enough to be visible to the naked eye. An example is differences in average height between 14- and 18-year-old girls. In contrast, the height difference between 15- and 16-year-old girls has an effect size of about .2. An effect size of .8 describes average differences in intelligence between Ph.D. recipients and typical college freshmen. (Box 3.4 presents a procedure for interpreting effect sizes.)

Such examples offer only rough guidelines. We caution against adopting absolute rules for judging the magnitude of effects. Whether an effect is large enough to matter depends upon the specific goals of a program or treatment (See Glass, McGaw, and Smith, 1981, pp. 99–106). Sometimes we want to choose among several program versions. The goal is then to identify the one with the biggest effect. Other times the precise size of an effect is less important. We may simply want to know if a treatment has a positive overall effect, or we may want to know that a program generally will not harm people.

---

**BOX 3.4.   ARE SMALL AVERAGE EFFECT SIZES RELEVANT TO POLICY?**

Rosenthal and Rubin (1982a) have developed a simple procedure for converting an estimate of effect size into a tabular display (Binomial Effect Size Display, or BESD) to show real-world importance more directly. The basic idea is to cast the relationship in a two-by-two table, making it easy to visualize. The strength of the relationship in the table is determined by the size of the effect. For example, suppose that a special reading program reduces the proportion of children needing tutoring compared to the old standard but that an evaluation using correlational analysis explains "only" 9 percent of the total variation. This effect can be displayed as follows, using Rosenthal and Rubin's procedure:

### READING PROGRAM

| Needs special tutoring | Special | Usual |
|---|---|---|
| Yes | 35 | 65 |
| No | 65 | 35 |

Effects that appear trivially small using standard indices such as *r* can have strong practical significance: "Employment of the BESD has, in fact, shown that we are doing considerably better in the behavioral and social sciences than we thought we were" (Rosenthal, 1983, p. 12).

For example, we may not expect long-term daycare to enhance young children's social development, but we would worry if its average impact turned out to be detrimental.

Judging the value of any program is easier if similar innovations provide points of comparison. For example, a good yardstick for a new teaching program is the success of its recent competitors (Walberg, 1983). If special tutoring using computers raises reading scores by an average effect of .8 while most other programs do no better than .5, we should be encouraged. Research reviews of several competing versions of a program can help to clarify the picture of usual effect sizes. It will also make the unusual easier to spot.

Averaging effect sizes has several drawbacks worth remembering. One is that ten studies all with effects of .3 produce the same average as nine studies at 0 and an outlier at 3.0. So a reviewer must decide whether averaging makes sense when outliers exist (see Box 3.5). A second is that small effects may be missing because of publication bias. This dilemma is not easily resolved. Even with a serious effort to locate unpublished studies, a reviewer should recognize the possibility that estimates of treatment impact will be inflated.

Should all studies contribute equally to an average? The simplest strategy is "one study–one effect." Compute a sim-

---

**BOX 3.5.   AVERAGES CAN BE MISLEADING**

We have cautioned against relying on an average effect size when there is an unusual distribution of study outcomes. An illustration for this caveat comes from Burger's (1981) review of studies examining the relationship between the severity of an accident and assigning responsibility for it. Burger identified 22 studies that exposed participants to different descriptions of accidents and assessed the impact of the severity of the described accident on the extent to which people held the perpetrator responsible. A partial summary of his results appears in Table C.

Notice that only 7 of the 22 studies provide sufficient information to compute an effect size (column "$d$" in the table). Six of these studies show positive effects (the group receiving more severe accident de-

TABLE C. MAIN EFFECT FOR RESPONSIBILITY OF PERPETRATOR
IN A NEGATIVE ACCIDENT.

| Author | Year | $n$ | $p$ | $z$ | $d$ |
|---|---|---|---|---|---|
| Walster | 1966 | 88 | .01 | 2.576 | .64 |
| Walster | | | | | |
|     Experiment 2 | 1967 | 95 | .50 | 0 | 0 |
| Shaver | | | | | |
|     Experiment 1 | 1970 | 55 | .50 | 0 | 0 |
|     Experiment 1 | 1970 | 19 | .50 | 0 | 0 |
|     Experiment 3 | 1970 | 40 | −.15 | 1.440 | −.53 |
| Shaw & Skolnick | 1971 | 58 | .50 | 0 | 0 |
| McKillip & Posavac | 1972 | 38 | .50 | 0 | 0 |
| Phares & Wilson | 1972 | 80 | .005 | 2.813 | 4.01 |
| Chaikin & Darley | 1973 | 40 | .50 | 0 | 0 |
| Schiavo | 1973 | 29 | .50 | 0 | 0 |
| Wortman & Linder | 1973 | 113 | .50 | 0 | 0 |
| Ugwuegbu & Hendrick | 1974 | 480 | .04 | 2.054 | .19 |
| McKillip & Posavac | | | | | |
|     Experiment 2 | 1975 | 64 | .50 | 0 | 0 |
| Medway & Lowe | 1975 | 42 | .05 | 1.960 | .48 |
| Shaw & McMartin | 1975 | 80 | .50 | 0 | 0 |
| Gleason & Harris | 1976 | 192 | .0005 | 3.591 | .57 |
| Lowe & Medway | 1976 | 120 | .001 | 3.291 | .64 |
| Schroeder & Linder | 1976 | 96 | .50 | 0 | 0 |
| Whitehead & Smith | 1976 | 162 | .50 | 0 | 0 |
| Pliner & Cappell | 1977 | 112 | .50 | 0 | 0 |
| Shaw & McMartin | 1977 | 160 | .50 | 0 | 0 |
| Younger, Earn, & | | | | | |
|     Arrowood | 1978 | 39 | .50 | 0 | 0 |

Source: Adapted from Burger (1981).

scriptions held the perpetrator more responsible), while one effect was negative. The effect sizes are .64, .19, .48, .57, .64, 4.01, and −.53, with an average of .86.

This example illustrates what can happen when the key summary statistic for a review is simply an average. The effect size of .86 is not inaccurate in any formal sense; it is indeed the correct mean of the seven scores. As Burger notes, however, the one unusually large effect dramatically inflates the mean; the average with this score excluded is .33. The value .86 does not characterize either the six more moderate effects or the one extreme outcome. It is unlikely that all seven sample values estimate the same underlying population value. Many readers will be more interested in why one study demonstrated such a huge effect, out of line with the others.

ple effect size for each study, and average them. But seeing that studies differ in important ways, such as sample size, a reviewer may choose to weight the effects accordingly. For example, rather than counting a study with 1000 participants the same as a study with 10 participants, the reviewer could weight the two effects according to some direct function of sample size. Mosteller and Bush (1954) offer techniques that accomplish this. These weighting procedures are not limited to sample size. They can be adapted, for example, to experts' ratings of the quality of studies.

In the end, the most important consideration in assessing the value of averaging effect sizes is whether or not this method answers the question motivating a review. (Box 3.6 shows how choice of summary measure can make a difference.) After all, characterizing an entire field of study with one number is extreme reduction of information. Its simplicity is appealing. But if averaging does not yield full enough answers, a reviewer should pursue some of the suggestions that follow.

---

**BOX 3.6.   COMPARING INDICES OF OVERALL TREATMENT IMPACT**

Does the choice of an overall index really make a difference? A recent review by Johnson et al. (1981) compared three indices of overall treatment impact: vote counting, averaging effect sizes, and combining significance tests. The authors reviewed studies looking at the impact on productivity of cooperative, competitive, and individualistic organizational strategies. Their goal was to see whether individual or group reward systems are most likely to enhance productivity in industry. We reproduce a partial quantitative summary in Table D.

Notice that the review is organized around six sets of paired comparisons, such as competitive versus individualistic approaches. These analyses offer some insight into the relative benefits of the three summary methods.

Conclusions from the different methods are reasonably congruent for some comparisons. For instance, cooperative programs clearly outper-

TABLE D.   THREE SUMMARY PROCEDURES.

| | Method | | | | | | |
| Conditions | Voting | | | Effect size | | | z Score | |
| | N | ND | P | M | SD | N | z | N |
|---|---|---|---|---|---|---|---|---|
| Cooperative vs.<br>group competitive | 3 | 6 | 4 | .00 | .63 | 9 | .16 | 13 |
| Cooperative vs.<br>competitive | 8 | 36 | 65 | .78 | .99 | 70 | 16.00 | 84 |
| Group competitive vs.<br>competitive | 3 | 22 | 19 | .37 | .78 | 16 | 6.39 | 31 |
| Cooperative vs.<br>individualistic | 6 | 42 | 108 | .78 | .91 | 104 | 24.01 | 132 |
| Group competitive vs.<br>individualistic | 1 | 10 | 20 | .50 | .37 | 20 | 11.37 | 29 |
| Competitive vs.<br>individualistic | 12 | 38 | 9 | .03 | 1.02 | 48 | 4.82 | 50 |

Source: Adapted from Johnson et al. (1981).
Note: N = negative; ND = no difference; P = positive.

form individualistic programs regardless of summary method. Other conclusions, however, vary depending upon the reviewing procedure. For example, the third pairing in the table shows how a mistaken conclusion can arise from a simple vote count. Of 44 statistical comparisons, 19 favor "group competitive" approaches, 3 favor "competitive" approaches, and 22 show no significant difference. While the no-effect category wins by a slim plurality, half of the tests reached statistical significance. Clearly this proportion far exceeds chance, as confirmed both by the highly significant overall probability estimate ($Z = 6.39$, $p < .00001$) and the fairly large average effect size (.37).

The bottom pairing in the table illustrates a different point: the questionable interpretation of a significant overall $p$ when large numbers of studies are combined. Comparisons of competitive versus individualistic strategies produce a minuscule average effect (.03) and a clear no-effect winner in the vote count. Yet the combined significance test turns out to be highly statistically significant (favoring competition), with $p$ less than .001. This reflects the fact that even very small effects, sometimes having little substantive importance, often turn up statistically significant when they are based on very large combined sample sizes. Reviewers should keep this caveat firmly in mind.

## Examining Variation in Study Outcomes

It is always a good idea to look at differences among study findings. Doing so helps us to understand the value of different summary methods. We can ask, do study outcomes differ by more than simple chance fluctuations (or sampling error)? Answering yes to this question strengthens the case for using measures that explain the variation rather than measures giving a single summary number. A second reason for focusing on outcome variation is that *substantive* questions might emphasize a search for differences among studies rather than for averages. In this section we present techniques useful in both situations: when variation is examined before computing an average, and when the variation itself is the main focus of interest.

### One Population of Studies, or Several?

A question every review should consider is whether the various studies are independent samples from the same underlying population, or from several distinct populations. Are the different studies really measuring the same thing?

For just about any collection of studies, outcomes will vary. Indeed, the chance of 20 studies all producing exactly the same result is so low that were it to happen, it would be suspect. How might we think about variation among findings?

One possibility is that variability among findings is purely *sampling error*. Even when many studies come from a single population, some chance differences in results will show up. This variation should be mathematically predictable, and exists because each study is only a small sample from a large population.

A second possibility—given different scientists working independently at different places at different times using different design and analysis strategies—is that conflicts come about because of *variations in the research process*. There may be a single underlying treatment effect, but systematic differences in *how* the effect is investigated may lead to divergent findings.

A third possibility is that studies correctly represent a world where a treatment has various underlying effects. Different outcomes are not attributable to sampling variation or to different research designs. Rather, they accurately represent reality. It is no surprise that some programs do not have a single, universal effect. Sometimes a program works particularly well in certain circumstances and less well elsewhere. Its value depends upon who participates, how the program is implemented, and so on.

A concrete example of this is reported by Raudenbush (1983), who reviewed 18 controlled studies examining the impact of teachers' expectations on pupils' IQ. Educators often disagree about the importance of teachers' expectations on students' test scores. Based on prior theory Raudenbush divided the 18 studies into two groups according to how long teachers and students knew each other (more than two weeks versus two weeks or less) before the teachers' expectations were manipulated. This simple division explained a substantial fraction of the variation in outcomes ($r = .77$). Raudenbush's findings illustrate how a group of studies that have different ways of implementing a treatment can be reinterpreted as coming from more than one population. Identifying the feature that discriminates among the populations, in this case *when* expectations were introduced, can clarify seemingly conflicting outcomes. We have several suggestions for determining if a group of studies comes from one or several populations.

### Identifying Overlapping Distributions

A good first step is to examine outcome distributions. Look at a simple frequency distribution of outcomes and a funnel display relating outcomes to sample size. One way to analyze an unusual distribution of outcomes is to classify studies according to a potentially important background characteristic. For example, classify according to average income of participants, low and high. Then plot the two (or more) sets of studies on the same graph. If the background variable is indeed important, the pattern of findings should be clarified dramatically. For example, a roughly bimodal overall distribution may divide into two distinct but overlapping distributions.

### Statistically Testing Homogeneity of Outcomes

A second approach is more formal and precise than visual displays: conduct a statistical test examining how much study results differ. The test compares the actual variation in outcomes to what would be expected simply because of *sampling error*. If the actual variation significantly exceeds chance, the idea that all studies come from the same population is discarded as unlikely.

Several authors present methods for examining variation formally (Hedges, 1982; Hunter, Schmidt, and Jackson, 1982; Rosenthal and Rubin, 1982b). Rosenthal and Rubin derive the test statistic

$$\chi^2 = \sum_{j=1}^{k} w_j \, (d_j - \bar{d})^2$$

where $k$ is the number of studies being combined, $d_j$ is the effect size in the $j$th study, $\bar{d}$ is the weighted mean effect size across studies, and $w_j$ is the weight applied to the $j$th result.[1] For modestly large sample sizes, the statistic has a chi-square distribution with $k - 1$ degrees of freedom. The idea is straightforward. On the one hand, if individual effect sizes

---

[1] In this formula,

$$\bar{d} = \sum_{j=1}^{k} \frac{w_j d_j}{\sum_{j=1}^{k} w_j}, \quad \text{and } w_j = \frac{(n_{1j} n_{2j})/(n_{1j} + n_{2j})}{1 + t_j^2/2(n_{1j} + n_{2j} - 2)}$$

where $n_{1j}$ and $n_{2j}$ are the sample sizes of the two groups in the $j$th study. See Rosenthal and Rubin (1982) or Hedges (1982) for full derivations. Hedges gives an $H$ statistic similar to that given by Rosenthal and Rubin.

vary dramatically around their mean, differences between $d_j$ and $\bar{d}$ will be large. The $\chi^2$ statistic will then be large. Large observed values indicate significant heterogeneity. On the other hand, if the $d_j$'s are all similar to $\bar{d}$, the resulting $\chi^2$ will be small and heterogeneity is unlikely. In the extreme case where all effects are almost the same, all $d_j$ are roughly $\bar{d}$, and variation among studies is practically zero. A reviewer who finds this extreme may be pleased, since the results from different studies agree perfectly. But a caution is in order: Are the findings too good to be true? Even when several studies turn up congruent results, sampling error should create at least a little variation. Finding no variation at all should make a reviewer suspicious.

Why are tests of the homogeneity of effect sizes important? Because finding significant heterogeneity raises a warning flag for a reviewer. In most reviews the goal is to combine studies that measure the same thing, be it the effect of aspirin tablets, presurgical intervention, or a job training program. If outcomes from several studies differ enormously, it becomes harder to believe the underlying treatments are really similar. So when this happens a critical question is *why* significant outcome differences exist. Shortly we will suggest how to answer this.

What if findings do *not* vary by more than predictable sampling error? Then we can be far more confident in a single, broad conclusion using all the studies (Hunter, Schmidt, and Jackson, 1982). Rather than shopping around for background factors to explain real differences among findings, we can focus the analysis more sharply on main effects.

It is terribly important to be cautious about accepting the *absence* of significant heterogeneity as definitive. The worry here is similar to cautions about "accepting the null hypothesis" in all statistical analysis. Not identifying significant variation in effect sizes is a far weaker conclusion than believing with high probability that all studies really are the same. A heterogeneity test may not be powerful enough to pinpoint real differences among studies.

In our opinion, heterogeneity tests are more valuable as

warning flags of unusual variation than as a justification for focusing one's analysis only on main effects. For example, suppose that ten studies examine an educational activity and that the five most successful programs use highly trained teachers. If a one-shot heterogeneity test is not significant, we will be reluctant to conclude that training is definitely important. Yet this information is valuable for the person designing the eleventh study. At the early stages of science, new ideas and provocative research suggestions may contribute more than "definitive" tests based on just a few early studies.

A final point about heterogeneity tests. It is a good idea to supplement them with qualitative analyses of program descriptions. Once each of a group of research findings is standardized into an effect-size format, it becomes statistically possible, indeed almost too easy, to combine results across studies. If we rely solely on statistical criteria, we may think a group of studies are homogeneous when in fact they are substantively very different. This can create a real problem. The additional clout provided by combining dissimilar studies is unwarranted. As an extreme example, the average effects of psychotherapy (Smith and Glass, 1977) and teachers' expectations (Rosenthal and Rubin, 1978) are quite similar: they are both approximately .6. Yet it would be nonsense to combine these two data sets simply because of the numerical resemblance. Conceptual clarity is far more important than any numerical similarity. Being sure that studies in a review are similar substantively as well as statistically is absolutely essential.

### Relating Background Variables to Outcomes

Suppose a visual display or homogeneity test identifies unusual variation in outcomes. Or suppose a substantive question focuses on interactions rather than main effects. Then a reviewer must try to explain when, or for whom, the outcomes are best. A first step is to code information about program characteristics, such as duration, intensity, or type of recipient. This information can then be tied to numerical outcomes in one of two ways: (1) by forming subgroups of studies based on substantive criteria and comparing average effect sizes among groups; or (2) by conducting regression analyses that use background characteristics such as type of program or type of participant to predict effect sizes. Glass, McGaw, and Smith (1981) and Hedges and Olkin (1982) give formulas for these regressions. They are direct extensions of regression procedures for a single study.

An example of dividing studies into groups using substantive criteria is Hall's (1978) review of sex differences in decoding nonverbal cues. First Hall found that women usually do better than men on such tasks. Then she divided studies into three groups representing three different communication modalities—visual only, auditory only, and visual plus auditory. Finally she computed an average effect size for each group. They are .32, .18 and 1.02 respectively. The third modality has a noticeably larger average effect than the other two. Hall suggests that this may be due to greater realism and precision of measurement in the visual plus auditory studies. (While Hall had no a priori prediction about how modalities would differ, some reviewers will make such predictions. For example, one might hypothesize that recent studies will show the largest program effects. Rosenthal [1983; Rosenthal and Rubin, 1982b] gives procedures for testing specific contrasts of this sort.)

An example of using regression is Smith and Glass's (1977) review of the effects of psychotherapy. The authors used regression analysis to assess what circumstances were related to the effectiveness of psychotherapy. For example, regression identified the amount of time elapsed between the end of therapy and the assessment of the patient as important. Figure 3.14 shows this relationship for approximately two hundred studies of systematic desensitization therapy (Glass, 1977). The measured value of therapy declines with longer time lags. Of course, this post hoc analysis must be interpreted carefully, since time lag is only one of many design characteristics varying across studies. One solution to

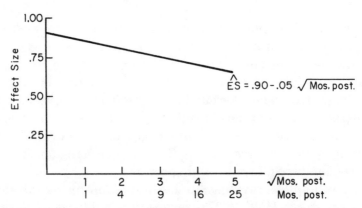

Figure 3.14. Regression of psychotherapy effect onto the time (square root of months) elapsing between therapy and assessment of outcomes for systematic desensitization therapy (from Glass, 1977).

this problem is statistical: background variables other than time lag can be controlled by including them in the regression (Glass, McGaw, and Smith, 1981). However, since the analysis is correlational, strong causal inferences are unwarranted.

Regression analysis is especially useful for identifying which background variables (such as time lag following psychotherapy) are important predictors of study outcomes. But remember to be cautious when generalizing from *studies* to individual *people*. The job training examples mentioned in Chapter 2 illustrate this. Job training programs with longer average training times could report lower average incomes for participants, even though individuals within all programs benefit financially from longer training. This would happen if programs providing the highest average hours of training are in the poorest neighborhoods, where participants need a lot of training to secure even low-paying jobs. Programs in richer areas might supply, on average, less training. But within each setting people receiving more training would do better. We stress this difference because public policies are designed to affect people rather than studies. So it is important to see if findings across studies also apply to individuals within studies.

## Identifying Unusual Outcomes

A different strategy for explaining discrepant findings is to single out extremes for intensive analysis. This follows Klitgaard's (1978) suggestion "to use the unusual as a guide to the usual, since the unusually successful (or unsuccessful) may provide a clearer picture of processes operating to a lesser extent elsewhere" (p. 531). To do this well, we must be able to identify *truly* unusual performances. (See also Canner, Huang, and Meinert, 1981a, 1981b.) For contrasting views on outliers, see Box. 3.7.

The simplest way to identify exceptional programs is to construct a frequency distribution of outcomes. Outcomes in the tails of the distribution can then be examined further. For instance, one may decide to look closely at the top and bottom 2 percent of outcomes. Comparing highly successful and unsuccessful programs may turn up several potentially important differences in structure. For example, unusually successful Head Start programs may have particularly high levels of parent participation.

After identifying potential explanatory factors from outliers, a reviewer can form specific hypotheses about how they influence a broader range of outcomes. These hypotheses can be examined in two ways. One is to evaluate them using data from less extreme studies. For example, if parent involvement in Head Start is universally important, there should be some evidence of this across the entire range of study outcomes. In fact, since public policies or regulations will often influence the usual more than the extreme, this step can be critical.

A second way of examining these hypotheses is to build them into future controlled experiments. Potentially important variables identified post hoc from existing programs can sometimes be varied systematically in a future experiment. The National Day Care Study (Ruopp et al., 1979) provides an illustration. The Administration for Children, Youth, and Families (ACYF) analyzed many studies of daycare curricula in 1974. This helped to isolate three key policy variables as

---

**BOX 3.7. TWO APPROACHES TO OUTLIERS**

When facing a large number of studies, a reviewer might adopt one of two quite different attitudes toward outliers, or outcomes that are extreme on either the high or low end. One attitude is to consciously *seek them out*. This might happen because a treatment, say a drug, has been tried in many settings, and the goal of a review is to see if there is any setting in which the treatment is extraordinarily effective or harmful. In this case, outliers carry the most important information in the entire review.

An example comes from educational research. Kippel (1981) looked at many schools and isolated extreme successes. He then examined each outlier in more detail, to see why certain schools were especially effective in educating their students:

> The main objective of the study was to identify schools that had made exceptional progress. Therefore, . . . only indices that were at least plus or minus one standard deviation from the mean were identified for each grade. This was accomplished by calculating the mean and standard deviation of the residuals for each grade. In our example, the means and standard deviations were .182 and 1.360, .193 and 2.027, and .154 and 1.946 for grades three, four, and five, respectively. This information was used to obtain cut-off points that were plus or minus one standard deviation from each mean . . . Only residuals below or above one standard deviation were considered in subsequent analyses. *In effect, any residual within one standard deviation of the mean was excluded from further consideration"* [emphasis added].

TABLE E.  EARNINGS GAINS BY SEX, MINORITY STATUS, AND TYPE OF TRAINING (IN 1980 DOLLARS).

|  | Women | Men |
|---|---|---|
| Minority participants | 1,000 | 600 |
| In classroom training | 1,100 | 300 |
| In on-the-job training | 800 | 1,500 |
| In work experience | 900 | 300 |
| Nonminority participants | 1,300 | −100 |
| In classroom training | 1,300 | 300 |
| In on-the-job training | 1,200 | −200 |
| In work experience | 1,400 | −300 |

*Source:* U.S. Congressional Budget Office (1982).

A different attitude toward outliers might be adopted by a reviewer who wants to focus on *central tendency*. In this case, outlying values are simply atypical occurrences and hold no special interest. An example of this comes from research on the CETA job training and placement program. A research review undertaken jointly by the Congressional Budget Office and the National Commission for Employment Policy examined gains in earnings, broken down by two background variables (participant's sex and minority status) and also by type of training received. Their summary findings are presented in Table E.

Most readers scanning the sixteen means in Table E will quickly spot the one obvious outlier, the minority men in on-the-job training. But since the purpose of this study was to report "typical" rather than exceptional or idiosyncratic results, here is how CBO chose to describe these data:

> There was no consistent pattern in the observed differences in the effect of training for minority and non-minority persons. Both minority and non-minority female participants experienced large future earnings gains, with some evidence of a smaller gain for minority women. But in five out of six cases, there was no significant effect for minority or non-minority male participants. The one exception to this rule—on-the-job training for minority males—produced the largest earnings gain for any group examined . . . Because this result was based on the experience of only 130 participants (representing 4 percent of the sample) and because it was inconsistent with virtually all other findings in this paper, it should be interpreted with caution.

distinguishing the best centers from the worst: staff-to-child ratio, staff training, and group size. ACYF then funded a large investigation. It included both a randomized field trial and an observational study, centered around these three variables. The results were that one (group size) was extremely important, one (staff training) was moderately important, and the last (staff-to-child ratio) was quite marginal. This effort illustrates the potential benefits of first generating hypotheses using outliers and then building better follow-up investigations that formally test the hypotheses.

As informative as outliers can be, several caveats are important. First, some study outcomes will appear in the tails of a distribution because of chance alone. This is a simple but often ignored idea (Hunter, Schmidt, and Jackson, 1982). After all, in any group of outcomes there is bound to be a largest and a smallest, even if there is nothing special about them. By singling out some studies just because they are at the top or bottom, we run the risk of *overcapitalizing on chance:* the programs may not be *really* special. The clues they provide about what causes programs to succeed or fail may lead to dead ends. For this reason, we view the analysis of outliers as an *exploratory* aid. It provides ideas rather than definitive tests. Second, specific features of programs are only one possible set of reasons for high or low performance. Background variables such as participant characteristics and geographic location can also have an impact. A school's exceptional test scores may be due primarily to exceptionally talented students rather than to any special academic program.

Klitgaard (1978; Kiltgaard and Hall, 1977) addresses precisely these issues in his search for exceptional schools. He points out that many factors other than school curriculum can influence student performance:

You wish to evaluate each school's average achievement score after adjusting for these nonschool differences. Following a common procedure in educational evaluation, you may decide to control for nonschool factors using regressional analysis. The difference between a school's actual score and the score predicted for it by the regression equation might then be used as a measure of the school's average achievement, given its students' different nonschool backgrounds" (1978, pp. 538–539).

Constructing a distribution based on these "residuals" helps us to focus on a program's effect. Figure 3.15 shows a frequency distribution of school effects, *after* controlling for SES, racial composition, and community type. Klitgaard uses histograms of residuals to pinpoint unusually successful schools: "The right tail of the histogram is of keen interest. If it is very thick, it may imply that more schools than one

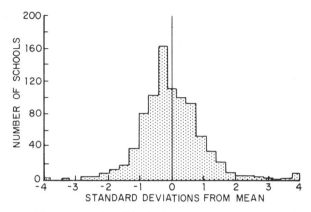

Figure 3.15. Histogram of residuals for 1970–1971 Michigan seventh-grade mathematics test, from a regression controlling for racial composition, community type, and socioeconomic status (from Klitgaard and Hall, 1977).

would expect are performing far above average. A long tail, stretching out to four, five, and six standard deviations above the mean, is evidence that some schools are extremely high achievers" (Klitgaard and Hall, 1977, p. 56).

After computing and displaying residuals, it is worth comparing the actual distribution with that predicted by chance fluctuations alone (see Klitgaard and Hall, 1977). If the number of very high or very low scores is unusually large, we may suspect that the outliers are "real" (not due simply to random variation). The next step is to analyze characteristics of the exceptional programs, to identify common features. For example, Klitgaard and Hall found that exceptional schools tended to have smaller classes, more experienced teachers, and higher teacher salaries than average schools. Klitgaard and Hall conclude that these analyses are equivocal—they require several statistical assumptions—but that the identified schools "deserve detailed study at the local level" (p. 81). We agree. While one is never certain that programs identified in this fashion are *truly* exceptional, the virtue of this analysis is that "it helps the scholar and policymaker know where to focus their attention" (Klitgaard, 1978, p. 546). Box 3.8 provides an example.

---

**BOX 3.8.   OUTLIERS CAN LEAD TO SUBSTANTIVE INSIGHTS**

Hall's (1978) data on sex differences in decoding nonverbal cues give an example of examining unusual outcomes for substantive insights. The following list presents effect sizes adapted from Hall's review:

| Effect size | Modality of communication | Effect size | Modality of communication |
|---|---|---|---|
| −.60 | V | .32 | A |
| −.31 | V | .34 | A |
| −.21 | A | .36 | V+A |
| −.17 | A | .38 | A |
| −.15 | V | .40 | V |
| −.14 | A | .40 | V |
| −.12 | V | .46 | V+A |
| −.02 | V | .48 | V |
| .00 | V | .53 | V |
| .00 | V | .54 | V |
| .02 | V | .56 | V+A |
| .03 | V | .60 | V |
| .03 | A | .61 | V+A |
| .05 | V | .65 | V |
| .10 | V | .67 | A |
| .11 | V | .67 | V |
| .14 | V | .69 | V |
| .14 | V | .78 | V+A |
| .26 | V | 1.02 | V |
| .29 | A | 1.12 | V+A |
| .30 | V | 1.31 | V |
| .30 | V | 1.86 | V |
| .31 | A | 3.28 | V+A |

While the distribution is reasonably symmetrical, there is one extremely high value (3.28), more than twice the size of all the other scores but one. What are the characteristics of this study that might set it apart? One distinguishing feature is modality of communication. This was one of only 7 studies that combined visual and auditory (V+A) modes—the other 39 used visual (V) or auditory (A) cues.

Notice that only the visual-plus-auditory distribution is composed entirely of positive effects, with an average of 1.02. Even with the outlier omitted, the average effect of this modality (.65) is over twice as large as the visual (.32) or auditory (.18) modalities. So here the outlier, 3.28, suggested that modality is a key background variable. This turned out upon further investigation to be a constructive suggestion. Hall identified a priori the potential importance of modality; in many other cases a post hoc analysis of extreme values will help a reviewer to understand the entire range of study outcomes.

---

## Special Problems of Quantitative Synthesis

This chapter has focused primarily on statistical procedures: computing effect sizes, conducting significance tests, regression analysis, and so on. The following three additional issues also come up in most quantitative reviews.

*Different outcome measures across studies.* Combining studies is easiest when they all use the same outcome measure. But given the diverse priorities and resources of different researchers, such uniformity is extremely rare. Take daycare as an example. Investigators have used various cognitive, physical, health, social, and emotional indices to assess its impact on participating children (Belsky and Steinberg, 1978).

When outcome measures differ, the reviewer faces a dilemma. Is it reasonable to combine across seemingly different measures? The problem is not primarily a technical one. Whenever means and standard deviations are available, effect sizes *can* be computed and averaged. Whether or not to do so is a substantive question. The answer is ultimately dictated by good sense rather than any rote formula. The key issue is conceptual clarity. Suppose a review of daycare findings includes cognitive measures for 3-year-olds in some studies and emotional measures for 6-year-olds in others. Then the reviewer must decide whether an overall quantitative summary will be useful and substantively sound. Just throwing together disparate measures because the title of each study contains the word "daycare" can be foolish, no matter how statistically elegant or precise the review.

*Multiple measures within studies.* A second issue is how to treat studies that report more than one outcome. Take daycare again. Suppose some studies compare daycare and home-reared children on both cognitive and social development with several measures of each, while other studies rely on only a single index. How should we balance their respective contributions in a review?

One way is to compute a separate effect size for each measure within each study. A study comparing children in daycare to home-reared children on five different outcomes then contributes five effect sizes to the review. This approach disaggregates the unit of analysis to each *comparison* rather than to each *study*. It uses all available information. But perhaps an unintended consequence is that studies with multiple measures will be weighted more heavily than those with only one or two. Also, several comparisons within any study are not independent. They were done by one investigator on one group of participants. This could lead to repeated bias.

One solution is to categorize outcomes by what they measure—such as emotional, social, or cognitive abilities—and then conduct separate analyses for each subgroup. However, since many studies use more than one cognitive measure, or emotional measure, this might not always be sufficient.

A second solution treats each study as the unit of analysis, and gives each study equal weight. It involves computing a "grand" effect for each study by averaging across the several measures (e.g., Kulik and Kulik, 1982). This way each study rather than each comparison gets one "vote" in the review. The tradeoff here is loss of information within studies.

We recommend following and reporting *both* procedures. This will expand a final report. But since averaging within studies requires computing effects for individual comparisons anyway, presenting both analyses minimally raises costs. Doing both allows a reader to explore any differences between analyses. For instance, suppose a large average effect size emerges from a summary using each comparison as a unit of analysis. Then we can ask whether such findings depend unduly on one or two studies with multiple measures.

*Missing numbers.* A quantitative review is impossible unless studies report the necessary statistical information. Data requirements for computing effect sizes are minimal. All we need are means and standard deviations, *or* exact test statistics such as $t$ and sample sizes. Yet it is surprising how often this information is unavailable. Some might even change the word surprising to shocking. For example, in our own work we recently looked at 24 studies of daycare's effect on children's intellectual development. Over half did not report sufficient information for computing simple effect sizes.

What are a reviewer's options when confronted with missing or insufficient data? One is to try to obtain missing information directly from authors. Since the statistics needed are quite basic—means and standard deviations—one would expect such efforts to be successful. The chance of success probably depends quite idiosyncratically upon the field, the investigators, and other factors such as how dated the studies are.

A second strategy is to fill in conservative estimates of effect sizes when studies have missing data. Usually this means assigning effect sizes of zero (see Box 3.9). The logic goes as follows: We do not know the treatment effect when statistics are missing. So if we plug in a zero we are assuming minimum treatment effect. If, despite this policy, the review shows the treatment to be effective, we can be confident that this overall conclusion would not change even if missing statistics were available.

This seemingly conservative strategy, however, is not always conservative. It depends upon your point of view. In some cases, such as research on the impact of daycare, or deinstitutionalization of mental patients, or reduced cost reimbursement for hospitalization, finding no effect of the new program can be a happy outcome. We may not expect day-

**BOX 3.9. ARE QUANTITATIVE METHODS USEFUL WHEN DATA ARE SCARCE?**

Psychologists have conducted many studies to investigate whether men or women are more susceptible to social influence from peers. Maccoby and Jacklin (1974) reviewed 47 studies examining sex differences in conformity. Cooper (1979) examined a subgroup of 14 of these studies, all comparing the two sexes in their response to "persuasive communication." He then applied quantitative indices to these 14 studies, producing an average effect size and overall statistical significance level, or $p$ value. A partial summary of his results appears in Table F.

Only two of the 14 studies had detailed enough quantitative information to compute an effect size ($d$). All other studies simply reported a nonsignificant sex difference. Faced with the dilemma of what to do with these 12 studies, Cooper chose to estimate each missing effect as zero: "The best strategy for dealing with incomplete data reports is to assume

TABLE F. PERSUASIVE COMMUNICATION (ATTITUDE CHANGE) EXPERIMENTS.

| Author | Year | N | Maccoby & Jacklin's (1974) $p$ | Retrieved $z$ score | Retrieved $d$ index |
|---|---|---|---|---|---|
| Dean, Austin, & Watts | 1971 | 161 | .50 | .52 | .12 |
| Eagly & Telaak | 1972 | 118 | .50 | 0 | 0 |
| Greenbaum | 1966 | 100 | .50 | 0 | 0 |
| Insko | 1965 | 70 | .50 | 0 | 0 |
| Insko & Cialdini | 1969 | 152 | .50 | 0 | 0 |
| Linder, Cooper, & Jones | 1967 | 53 | .50 | 0 | 0 |
| Marquis | 1973 | 52 | .50 | 0 | 0 |
| Nisbett & Gordon | 1967 | 152 | .50 | 0 | 0 |
| Osterhouse & Brock | 1970 | 160 | .50 | 0 | 0 |
| Rosenkrantz & Crockett | 1965 | 176 | .50 | 0 | 0 |
| Rule & Rehill | 1970 | 90 | .50 | 0 | 0 |
| Silverman | 1968 | 403 | .50 | 1.41 | .16 |
| Silverman, Shulman, & Wiesenthal | 1970 | 98 | .50 | 0 | 0 |
| Worchel & Brehm | 1970 | 73 | .50 | 0 | 0 |
| $M$ | 1968.8 | 132.7 | .50 | .14 | .02 |

*Source:* Adapted from Cooper (1979).
*Note:* Positive $z$ values denote more female conformity.

an exact finding of no difference. Thus, such studies are treated . . . as having uncovered a *t* value of zero with a probability of .50. As meta-analysis combined probabilities become lower, we can assume that this procedure increases 'conservative' bias in our estimates and inferences'' (p. 139). Using this conservative substitution strategy, Cooper found the average effect size across 14 studies to be .02. By combining *z* scores, he found this sex difference to be not statistically significant.

These results illustrate the difficult choices confronting a reviewer when statistical information is scarce. Twelve of the 14 studies were assigned an effect size of zero. This was not done because studies found this exact value, but rather because the original research documents simply reported a nonsignificant difference between men and women. No one wants to throw away data. But there is a tradeoff: the effect estimate and combined probability lack precision. Some reviewers will find narrative information in research reports more informative than a statistical summary where all but two of the entries are inexact because of missing data.

---

care to raise IQs or to make children happier; we are satisfied if it simply does no harm. We rarely expect reducing costs to improve health; the goal is to not do it significant harm. In such cases, plugging in conservative statistics may bolster such an optimistic conclusion unjustifiably.

When effect sizes are not extractable from several studies, and when efforts to get this information directly from authors fails, it makes sense to focus quantitative analyses on the subgroup of studies with good information. Basing analyses on data that seem firm can only increase confidence in the review as a whole. Of course, this opens another question. If many studies do not have clear numerical findings, whether by design or not, can we still learn from them? This is a focal topic of the next chapter.

# NUMBERS AND NARRATIVE: THE DIVISION OF LABOR

# 4

Social scientists can be divided roughly into two broad camps: those who prefer qualitative case reports, and others who favor quantitative, statistically based studies. These different emphases are reflected in graduate training and professional publications. Major journals are categorized routinely either as "quantitative" or "qualitative." Of course there is some overlap, but serious efforts to integrate the different approaches are all too rare.

For years, the debate between proponents of "numbers" and those of "narrative" has focused on how to conduct individual studies (Reichardt and Cook, 1979). Proponents of case studies argue that most of what really matters in any real-world situation is nonquantifiable. Others see formal statistical description and hypothesis testing as the only road to rigorous science.

Does quantification lead to better science? The answer is unclear. Even distinguished statisticians find this question exceedingly complex:

All scientific knowing is indirect, presumptive, obliquely and incompletely corroborated at best. The language of science is subjective, provincial, approximate, and metaphoric, never the language of reality itself. The best we can hope for are well-edited approximations (Campbell, cited in Mahoney, 1976, p. 126).

The most important maxim for data analysts to heed, and one which many statisticians have shunned is this: Far better an approximate answer to the right question, which is often vague, than an exact answer to the wrong question, which can always be made precise (Tukey, 1962, p. 13).

The controversy has spilled over to research reviews. The hope (and promise) of statistical synthesis is to take most subjectivity, "art," and "personal stamp" out of reviews. Taken to an extreme, this seems not only ill-advised but impossible. The growth of quantitative procedures for analyzing data in single studies has not banished subjectivity, turned all investigators into good ones, or eliminated poor analyses. There still is a role for careful description, process analysis, insight, and creativity. Similarly, when quantitative procedures for aggregating findings are more firmly entrenched there will still be good and bad reviews, more skilled and less skilled reviewers. We believe the hard work of blending quantitative and qualitative information will be an important distinguishing factor.

In this chapter we develop a framework for thinking about case studies and qualitative data. This leads to a discussion about when different kinds of information have their special comparative advantages. It also leads to some specific suggestions for combining descriptive and statistical information in reviews. The overriding theme is that arguments about whether numerical or narrative reviews are intrinsically better lead nowhere. An "either or" position is neither necessary nor productive. Our general attitude is captured well by Cook and Leviton (1980), who argue that the best syntheses make the most out of both types of information:

What we have, then, is a difference in priorities about two types of questions, each of which has value. Science needs to know its stubborn, dependable, general "facts," and it also needs data-based, contingent puzzles that push ahead theory. Our impression is that meta-analysts stress the former over the latter, and that many qualitative reviewers stress the latter more than the former (or at least more than meta-analysts do). Of course, neither the meta-analyst nor the qualitative reviewer *needs* to make either prioritization. Each can do both; and any one reviewer can consciously use both qualitative and quantitative techniques in the same review. Indeed, s/he should (p. 468).

## Scientific Method versus Verstehen

Statistical and qualitative research strategies have characteristic strengths and weaknesses. The former predominates in contemporary science, so much so that the term "scientific method" is associated almost exclusively with *quantitative* methods. These scientific ideas include rigid experimental control, reliable and valid test instruments, probability sampling, and rigorous statistical analysis of data (Patton, 1975). For individuals working within this paradigm, there exist broad guidelines for scientific conduct. For example, Fisher's (1935) ideas about experimentation and Campbell and Stanley's (1966) discussion of alternative research designs have become the scripture of many evaluation specialists.

But there are tradeoffs. Statistical studies have real advantages, which they pay for with a serious limitation: an outcome that cannot be quantified reliably cannot be investigated. Researchers unhappy with this drawback favor an alternative approach, sometimes called "verstehen" (ver-stay'-hen: Patton, 1975; Scriven, 1966) or "illuminative evaluation" (Parlett and Hamilton, 1976). Here the goal is to reconstruct imaginatively the standpoint or perspective of people being studied. This gives their behavior concrete meaning. Verstehen is related to Stake's (1978) notion of "naturalistic generalization." A reader of research findings is able to identify with those who are studied, to draw analogies between his experience and theirs, and thus to understand their actions in a new way. The strength of verstehen is the depth of insight it permits. Its weakness, conversely, is that reliability and validity are difficult to assess. There are few widely agreed upon formal procedures for generating research findings in this way.

Which approach is more appropriate, statistical or verstehen, both for individual studies and for collections of such studies, depends upon both the research context and its ultimate purposes. If one wants to estimate how many children living in Detroit attend special education classes, or assess the effects of work release on criminal recidivism rates, or evaluate the impact of motorcycle helmet laws on serious accidents, traditional scientific assumptions usually are acceptable. But if one wants to know how individual children personally perceive special educational placements, or what motivates convicted felons to continue committing crimes, or why some individuals intentionally ignore motorcycle safety precautions, verstehen takes a reader beyond standard statistics. In such research there may be no expectation that other investigators would uncover exactly the same insights. Indeed, a study's unique value may lie in a particular scientist's special abilities and sensitivities. (As Box 4.1 shows, both types of research are common.)

Comparisons of the scientific method and verstehen imply the necessity of choice. Words and numbers are different "languages." So, for scientific communication to proceed, researchers must choose a mother tongue. Contributions of non-native speakers are either translated or ignored. Statistical analysis and case descriptions are polar opposites that coexist on a continuum; more of one must result in less of the other.

This attitude of forcing a choice rarely helps a reviewer. We believe it is far more constructive to view numbers and narrative as two *separate* dimensions (Light and Pillemer, 1982). Thus, any single study can be categorized independently along each, as in Figure 4.1. Similarly, a review need not be primarily quantitative or descriptive—it can be strong or weak on *both* dimensions.

Reviewers should work hard to build an *alliance* of both types of information. Each type offers unique benefits. To underscore the value of allying different kinds of evidence, we take a short theoretical detour into how people cumulate disparate information. This will help to clarify a *division of labor* between quantitative and case-study findings. The dis-

---

**BOX 4.1. SCIENTIFIC METHOD VERSUS ''WISDOM''
LITERATURE IN POLICY RESEARCH**

Schneider, Stevens, and Tornatzky (1982) present a content analysis of 181 randomly selected articles published in policy journals between 1975 and 1980. Interpreting their results is similar to the dilemma of whether the glass is half full or half empty.

. . . the typical article in the sampled literature is one of two fairly distinct types. Either it is a discussive, non-quantitative example of wisdom literature (e.g., armchair theorizing), or it is a more scientific, data-based piece. Clearly a bimodal distribution of method characterizes this field . . .

Further, 43 percent of the articles could be characterized as scientific or pre-scientific in nature. They tended to be empirical in nature, involved measurement of identifiable variables, tended to be quantitative, and usually had an identifiable research methodology. There is a minority interest in the community for the advancement of policy inquiry as science.

⁄ The more alarming discovery was that the policy journals are clearly dominated by wisdom literature; 57 percent of our sample contained few, if any, characteristics of ''science,'' even if one is quite liberal with that term. Our data suggest that the policy field has become divided into two prevailing types: the quantitative-empirical and the rhetorical-discussive (p. 111).

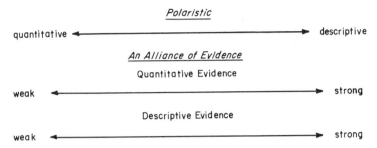

Figure 4.1. Two views of combining quantitative and descriptive information in a research synthesis.

tinction must be conceptually as well as methodologically sound. What is the appropriate domain for each? Where is each truly essential? Where should their influence overlap?

Answering these questions is important for two reasons. First, conceptual clarification is necessary to convince skeptics on both sides of the debate that calls for combining quantitative and qualitative insights are more than empty platitudes. Second, the answers lead to some concrete guidelines for reviewers.

## Using Different Kinds of Evidence

"After all, man is, in his ordinary way, a very competent knower, and qualitative commonsense knowing is not replaced by quantitative knowing. Rather, quantitative knowing has to trust and build on the qualitative, including ordinary perception. We methodologists must achieve an applied epistemology which integrates both" (Campbell, 1975, p. 191). In this passage, Campbell takes a first step in assigning "duties" to qualitative and quantitative information. Qualitative knowing is the foundation upon which statistical understanding must build. In what sense is qualitative information a building block for later quantitative work?

Part of the answer comes from theoretical work in psychology on *scripts*. Scripts have been used by Schank and Abelson (1977) among others to explain knowledge acquisition. The concept is straightforward and it is useful here. In dealing with the world, people encounter many situations. Some experiences are novel, but most are repeated over and over. For any recurring event, a person develops some general expectations about it. These expectations are scripts. An example is going to a restaurant. The first few visits may bewilder a young child. But soon a restaurant script develops. A waiter seats you at a table. A menu is presented before you order. Food is then delivered. You pay the check after you eat, and so on. When you go to a restaurant you routinely expect this sequence of events. There also are scripts for preparing dinner, teaching a class, going to a movie, writing a scientific paper, and so on.

Script formation helps people with *information management*. It sets guidelines for what is usual and routine versus what is new, disturbing, or memorable. For example, a highly scripted activity such as brushing your teeth is easy to execute. The expectations are simple, overlearned, and unambiguous. When such a mundane event takes place routinely, each new episode does not generate valuable new information, and therefore is "forgettable."

Many but not all life experiences confirm existing scripts. There are two major types of nonconfirmatory experience: (1) truly novel events, and (2) events that violate existing scripts. The first time a child enters a restaurant or an adult is interviewed for a job, the "rules" are largely unknown. Certainly they are not second nature. And even when scripts exist, new experiences can conflict with preconceptions. A waiter *could* ask you to pay before the food arrrives. Or pour the soup on your head. Or your car could break down on the way to work. With novel events, the specifics carry valuable information for guiding future actions until a generalized script is formed. With violations, recalling details of the anomaly also offers future guidance. For instance, you could avoid the offending restaurant and waiter. This might explain what restaurant managers, store owners, and others who deal with the public frequently observe: unexpected negative occurrences are often more memorable than pleasant but expected experiences.

Script theory provides a widely applicable model for the accumulation of knowledge. There are two basic types of knowledge: general, rule-governed, scripted information; and episodic, detailed, vivid records of specific events. When scripts govern behavior, information processing proceeds smoothly and efficiently. Details of particular experiences consistent with general expectations have little long-term value. However, when scripts are absent or violated, the value of episodic information increases dramatically.

## Scripts in Science

Scripts provide a useful, if somewhat limited, model of certain aspects of scientific knowledge. Repeatedly observing consistent patterns of empirical outcomes leads to general expectations or *paradigms*. If we repeatedly see that aspirin lowers fevers, or that social-class differences exist on standard IQ tests, the scientific community accepts these outcomes as general and robust. They become scripts for the future.

Research reviews play an obvious role in the script-building process. A primary function is to search for consistency among tens or hundreds of diverse studies. A review can tell us whether a coherent pattern exists. George Miller's (1956) classic paper about the "magical number seven" is a good example. Miller reviewed many studies of human problem solving. He noticed a pattern that suggests a finite limit on the amount of information any person can process at one instant—"seven plus or minus two" units. Miller wryly states that he has been "persecuted by an integer." His observation that the amount of available mental capacity is similar across different experiments and tasks provides an organizational framework, or script, for contemporary research on memory and problem solving. While all of the individual studies were available before 1956, it took Miller's insightful review to identify their intriguing consistency.

Once scripts are found, they are tied to systematic rules of scientific discovery. This can be reflected, for example, in the testing of null hypotheses. The hypothesis an investigator tests usually specifies *no* effect for a new or experimental treatment (say a new drug or curriculum) relative to an old one. This null hypothesis is tentatively "accepted" while the burden of empirical proof is placed on the innovation. Experimental results must be strong (or "highly statistically significant") in order to overthrow established scientific scripts. In this sense, our science is as conservative as our mental faculties. Nonsignificant results simply get swallowed by existing scripts. They are not memorable. They also are not highly valued by the scientific community and often suffer from journal publication bias (Greenwald, 1975). In contrast, extreme or unscripted results create more excitement. They elicit more interest and are more likely to be published, adding to the collective scientific memory. When an empirical finding violates current scientific expectations, qualitative details of the anomalous study become important and are reviewed with extra care.

### Scripts and Quantitative versus Qualitative Information

Script theory helps to explain the complementary roles of qualitative process studies on the one hand and quantitative hypothesis tests on the other. In the early stages of scientific exploration, a primary activity is "fact-gathering" (Kuhn, 1962, p. 15). Patterns are fleshed out by recording what is observed. It is too early for statistical hypothesis testing.

It is no coincidence that the pioneering research of psychologists such as Freud, Piaget, and Skinner consists largely of observational studies based on just a few individuals. Introductory students learn about the field's foundations from

Freud's Rat Man, Little Hans, and Dora; Piaget's observations of his own children; Skinner's work with a few white rats; and his predecessor Watson's conditioning studies with Little Albert. In psychology, at least, it is surprisingly hard to find a specific experiment with lasting impact. Yet there are critical observational studies. Such studies generate scripts and hypotheses for a wealth of follow-up quantitative work. At these later stages, global scripts are dissected and given specificity. Hundreds of empirical "tests" of Piaget's, Freud's, and Skinner's theories attest to this.

Qualitative observation, then, is the foundation of much scientific work. Does it also have a major role at later stages, after scientific scripts are well established? Indeed it does— one major role is in response to *script violations.* Imagine the stir that would be caused by a serious study reporting that aspirin raises fevers. When something like this happens, qualitative details of the renegade study become relevant to science, since there is no script to explain the anomaly. These details will guide future explorations to resolve the controversy.

Earlier qualitative studies also become salient again when current studies violate longstanding scientific scripts. An example is recent debate in psychology about a famous case study reported by Watson in 1920 (see Harris, 1979). Watson tried to provoke "conditioned fear" in a 9-month-old infant, Little Albert. He paired the presentation of a white rat with a loud, fearful sound. Soon presenting the rat without the sound elicited a fear response (the "conditioned" response). Later it was found that the fear had generalized to other stimuli such as a rabbit and a short-haired dog. This experiment is part of behaviorist folklore. It is used to explain conditioned emotional responses, stimulus generalization, and the origins of phobias. These have become important elements in learning theory scripts.

Some researchers ask, "Why this sudden upsurge of interest in Watson after all these decades?" (Harris, 1980). One answer is that this collective "reminiscence" was triggered by contemporary scientific developments. Recent empirical work leads to models of phobia formation that are different from Watson's (Harris, 1979, p. 155). The challenge to existing scientific scripts apparently has triggered a look back to the roots of traditional models. In addition, one new theory cites Watson's work as supporting evidence (Seligman, 1971). Evaluating the new theory involves questioning Watson's old data. So specific details of a case study several generations old become important again. Interestingly, the scientific collective memory is not always accurate. Details of Watson's original experiment frequently have been misrepresented in current writings (Harris, 1979).

A second example comes from the long-standing controversy over how to explain variation in performance on IQ tests. Proponents of heredity (e.g., Jensen, 1969; Munsinger, 1974, 1978) and of environment (e.g., Kamin 1974, 1978) have sparred repeatedly. While one line of this debate emphasizes generating "definitive" new research, early studies are also undergoing careful scrutiny. For example, studies by the geneticist Cyril Burt supporting hereditarian views have been reexamined in minute detail, and serious questions have been raised about the integrity of Burt's data. An influential book by Gould (1981) retraces the early history of genetic determinism. Century-old studies and data are reviewed and reworked. We do not give the heredity-environment example because we think we have a simple answer to this venerable debate. Rather, we believe it illustrates that one major response to conflict in contemporary views is a reexamination of our episodic roots. Clearly, one way that science evaluates whether a controversial script is sound is to check whether its foundation is firm.

Understanding script theory helps us to see how different kinds of information have complementary roles for accumulating knowledge. Many scripts develop initially from repeated observations. Qualitative studies are essential for this. Once established, scientific scripts can be examined by hypothesis testing. While this activity is primarily quantitative or statistical, qualitative information does not lose its value even at these later stages.

Some readers will find this view of science simplistic and overly inductive. We agree. The proposed chain of events—from simple observation to scripts to testable models—is only one of the ways science progresses. For example, some theories are advanced prior to (rather than as a result of) empirical demonstrations. We use this (intentionally limited) approach as a heuristic device for illustrating links between different forms of evidence.

When does qualitative information play its strongest comparative role? We see two main occasions. First, case studies are crucial *in the early stages of science, in the newer sciences, and in mature sciences when new phenomena arise;* that is, when scripts are forming. An overemphasis on quantitative methods at these junctures can be counterproductive. To force-fit statistical hypothesis testing where no script exists is to miss important qualitative steps.

Second, qualitative information is *a guide for action when scripts are violated, or when conflicts arise.* Conflicts among studies are quite common; most research reviews turn up findings that disagree (Jackson, 1980). Qualitative insights often help to resolve such conflicts. One example of this comes from medical research. Durlak (1979) reviewed 42 studies comparing physicians and nurse practitioners and concluded that for certain services "paraprofessionals achieve clinical outcomes equal to or significantly better than those obtained by professionals" (p. 80).

This result violated the expectations of the medical community. Several investigators (Lewis et al., 1974; Merenstein, Wolfe, and Barker, 1974) had obtained qualitative information about *why* the statistical comparisons came out as they did. These efforts revealed that nurses and physicians allocated their time differently and differentially weighed the importance of various symptoms and incidents. The qualitative insights prompted action: physicians have made some adjustments in their allocation of time.

# Nonquantitative Information in Literature Reviews

Specifying general circumstances when qualitative data are important leads to some concrete suggestions for using them in research reviews. We build upon the theme that science should pursue an alliance of numbers and narrative. In this spirit, we first identify five different sources of qualitative evidence, followed by seven reasons, with examples, why this information should "have a say" in reviews. Finally, we present several concrete suggestions for maximizing the benefits of both numerical and descriptive findings.

### Five Sources of Nonquantitative Evidence

In discussions of nonquantitative evidence, labels like "descriptive," "qualitative," and "narrative" appear almost interchangeably. These terms all refer to information that is not precisely quantitative, but conceptual clarity about what nonquantitative sources of information are available, and how to use them, is often missing. It is useful to distinguish more clearly among different types of nonquantitative evidence.

1. *Single case designs.* Detailed studies of single cases are common, and techniques for analyzing such information are rapidly being developed (Herson and Barlow, 1976; Kratochwill, 1977, 1978). Observation of single individuals has contributed heavily to the theories of Freud, Piaget, and Skinner—among the most influential social scientists. Dukes (1965) and Herson and Barlow (1976) present many examples of "$N = 1$" research in psychology. Case studies are used in public policy analysis to examine the effects of such nonexperimental events as political decisions by cities and towns (Yin and Heald, 1975). They are also used as historical lessons for guiding future policy. For example, the Federal Aviation Administration always examines the flight recorder after a commercial airplane mishap to learn not only what caused the mishap but also whether similar occurrences can

be avoided in the future. New regulations about the fire resistance of materials in airplane lavatories following a retrospective analysis of a fire aboard an airliner illustrate how a study of one historical case led to concrete policy change.

The term "case study" refers to an analysis of a single event, or to disaggregated studies of multiple events (Kennedy, 1979). Even if a case uses a quantitative outcome, it is not possible to compute an effect size in the traditional manner. If each person is viewed as constituting a separate study, there is no direct measurement of within-group variation and also no control group. A reviewer wishing to summarize such findings must look for alternative procedures (see Box 4.2).

2. *Nonquantitative aggregate studies.* Some research outcomes are difficult to measure objectively or numerically with satisfactory reliability. A clinical psychologist may report that weight loss often improves the lives of obese people or that hypnosis is effective in helping cancer patients adjust to chemotherapy. While an implicit baseline must exist for such statements, the benefits may not have been assessed with objective tests. In fact, an investigator may feel that the psychological effects of weight loss or hypnosis cannot be assessed accurately with a simple numerical measurement; verstehen is more appropriate than formal tests. A reviewer of such studies will want to include these nonquantitative insights.

A related situation occurs when quantitative studies do not contain sufficient information for statistical synthesis. For example, research with weak experimental designs may include some quantitative information. The reading performance of a group of children might be assessed with a standardized test following a special tutoring session. But without a comparison group an effect size cannot be computed. Other studies might compare a treatment group to a control, but do not report sufficient information for producing a statistical summary. We recently looked carefully at a series of investigations of the effects of daycare on children's intellectual development. We located 24 studies comparing children in daycare with home-reared children. Over half did not report enough information (means, standard deviations, sample sizes, or exact test statistics) to allow us to compute simple effect sizes. This leaves us with a choice: either omit these studies, or treat them in some nonquantitative manner.

---

### BOX 4.2. "QUANTIFYING" CASE STUDIES

Yin and his colleagues (Yin and Heald, 1975; Yin, Bingham, and Heald, 1976) offer a "case survey" method for quantifying case studies. Each study is rated on several dimensions, such as research quality, program characteristics, and outcomes. These multiple ratings are then cumulated across studies, providing an overall numerical summary. Scorers also indicate their level of confidence for each judgment, allowing for reliability comparisons of "sure" and "unsure" ratings.

Yin and Heald (1975) used this method in reviewing 269 case studies of urban areas following decentralization of services. They found that clients' attitudes toward services improved in approximately 25 percent of the cases. This finding held whether the raters were unsure or sure of their categorization of outcomes. These summaries are not rigorously quantitative, and so they cannot be combined directly with effect sizes or significance levels calculated from quantitative studies. But they indicate roughly the overall success of urban innovations in the case study literature. That success rate can then be compared with results from quantitative reviews.

A weakness of this "numberizing" is the loss of much rich descriptive detail. Yin and Heald (1975) clearly discuss the tradeoffs:

> The case survey method, in its focus on aggregating general lessons, may not give sufficient attention to the unique factors of an individual case. The trade-off here is similar to the trade-off between experimental and clinical research. Only the latter may provide a full appreciation of the individual case; the former, however, must be relied upon more heavily if the goal is to create generalizations about groups of individuals . . . The case survey method may be more appropriate where the primary concern is with assessment and not necessarily with the discovery of process (p. 380).

3. *Nonquantitative information in quantitative studies.* In preparing a research report, authors usually do not simply list numerical results. Treatments and participants are carefully described, caveats and limitations painstakingly laid out. Often the effort put into these nonquantitative descriptions far surpasses the work of the numerical analyses.

Quantitative reviews lean most heavily on numerical information. What about all the rest of each original study? Is it always appropriate or desirable to reduce a journal article to one or a few numerical indices? Can one number accurately represent the outcomes of a research study conducted over several months or years? Can it take into account attrition, changes in procedure, and a variety of unexpected or notable happenings? (See Box 4.3 for an example.) Most scientists would probably hesitate to ignore such information. Other solutions are necessary. For example, it is sometimes possible to code qualitative background information and relate it formally to quantitative outcomes.

4. *Expert judgment.* The decision to limit subjective input is itself subjective. Reviewers may wish to draw on the wisdom of researchers and practitioners who have intimate experience with a program or treatment. For example, a reviewer might incorporate expert evaluations of studies by weighting each study according to an expert's judgment of its overall value. Techniques that already exist for weighting the outcomes of individual studies by their sample size (Mosteller and Bush, 1954; Rosenthal, 1978) can be adapted to experts' ratings. This procedure helps to formalize what experts do when subjectively weighing the results of different studies to reach an overall conclusion. If an expert believes that a study provides especially strong evidence, the results from that study will receive extra weight. (Box 4.4 suggests how experts' ratings can be quantified.)

Incorporating experts' judgments can enrich a review. For example, one can compare syntheses using different experts' weightings, and then compare the various results with a simple unweighted analysis. This would explicitly mark the areas

---

**BOX 4.3. CHANGING DEFINITIONS OF TREATMENT AND CONTROL GROUPS**

Narrative information accompanying quantitative analysis is critical when definitions of what is a treatment group and what is a control group change over time. This is not common, but it has happened, especially when public policy considerations change rules governing what persons should get what services.

An example comes from studies of special education—special class placements for children who are physically handicapped, have low IQ, or have some other special need. Before the early 1970s, studies examining the effects of special-placement classes upon children defined these classes as the treatment, while children in regular classes were the controls. Then a reversal occurred. We quote from a National Academy of Sciences report by Heller, Holtzman, and Messick (1982):

> The increased role of the judiciary in special education, the growing disenchantment with segregated special classes among influential educators, . . . and the attendant restructuring of the laws governing the education of handicapped children led to a renewed interest in research on the effects of special education in the 1970s. The research addressed questions similar to those of the early efficacy literature, but the hypotheses of the later studies reflected a different bias. Children in the mainstreamed classes were now considered the experimental group and children in special classes the control. This shift was partially the result of provisions in Public Law 94-142, which require the placement of children in the least restrictive environment" (p. 262).

Without a careful qualitative analysis of special education efforts, a quantitative summary runs the risk of reversing treatment and control groups and hopelessly confusing the review.

---

**BOX 4.4. CAN EXPERTS' JUDGMENTS BE QUANTIFIED?**

Experts often are asked questions like: "How big a risk does daycare pose to an infant's emotional development?" or "Does viewing television violence cause aggression?" While it is possible in principle to give a precise numerical answer to such questions (for example, 10 percent chance of serious risk), experts may be hesitant to do that formally. They may prefer to supply judgments or assessments in a more familiar verbal fashion (it is "unlikely" that emotional development will be impeded, or it is "very possible" that television violence increases aggressive behavior).

Translating these judgments into precise probability estimates requires a sophisticated conversion system. Mosteller (1976) addresses this issue by drawing on a model developed by Cliff (1959). Mosteller reports a study by Selvidge (1972) that found that the median person in a sample of business students interpreted the word "possibly" to mean a 20 percent probability that an event would occur. Cliff provides numerical weightings for various adverbs, based on college students' judgments. Interestingly, the weights are surprisingly stable across different groups of respondents. Cliff proposes that an adverb (such as "very") has a multiplicative effect on the probability estimate of the adjective (such as "possible") it modifies. For example, the weighting or multiplicative effect of "very" is about 1.25. So the median estimate for an event that is "very possible" is 1.25 × .20, or 25 percent. As one would expect, a "very possible" event is deemed more likely to occur than an event that is simply "possible." Table G presents the multiplicative effect of selected adverbs on the adjective "possible."

TABLE G. MULTIPLICATIVE EFFECT OF SELECTED ADVERBS ON THE SUBJECTIVE PROBABILITY ASSOCIATED WITH THE ADJECTIVE "POSSIBLE."

| Adverb | Weight[a] | Probability estimates for modifications of "possible"[b] | |
|---|---|---|---|
| Slightly | .538 | Slightly possible | .538 × 20 = 11% |
| Somewhat | .662 | Somewhat possible | .662 × 20 = 13% |
| Rather | .843 | Rather possible | .843 × 20 = 17% |
| Pretty | .878 | Pretty possible | .878 × 20 = 18% |
| Quite | 1.047 | Quite possible | 1.047 × 20 = 21% |
| Decidedly | 1.165 | Decidedly possible | 1.165 × 20 = 23% |
| Very | 1.254 | Very possible | 1.254 × 20 = 25% |
| Unusually | 1.281 | Unusually possible | 1.281 × 20 = 26% |
| Extremely | 1.446 | Extremely possible | 1.446 × 20 = 29% |

Source: Light and Pillemer, 1982.
a. Weights were obtained from Cliff's (1959) Princeton sample.
b. The probability estimate of 20% for "possible" was obtained from Mosteller (1976).

Future work in testing and extending Cliff's model will ultimately determine its validity. Using a simple multiplicative model to capture a complex judgment clearly provides no final answer. Yet we believe it is an intriguing beginning toward systematically using the judgments of many experts.

where experts disagree. If certain studies are rated positively by some experts and negatively by others, the discrepancies should be explored. Lack of agreement may pinpoint methodological, substantive, or ideological issues that lie at the core of the controversy. When evaluations by experts are consistent, we can be more confident about the innovation under investigation.

5. *Narrative reviews of collections of research studies.* Supporters of quantitative procedures have focused on the negative aspects of traditional narrative reviews. While many of these points are well taken, narrative reviews are not *by definition* full of flaws. Cook and Leviton (1980) argue this point convincingly. A careful narrative review becomes especially valuable when the author makes explicit a rationale for any analytic procedures that were used. Indeed, such narrative reviews may even provide useful information for statistical summaries.

### Why Nonquantitative Information Should Have a Say

"Investigators tend to pursue only those questions which can be easily evaluated by null hypothesis testing, and they will favor those which are most likely to yield results which are statistically significant (versus epistemologically relevant). This may encourage what Mitroff and Featheringham call 'the fallacy of misplaced precision' or Type III error—having solved the wrong problem" (Mahoney, 1976, p. 102). These comments reflect the belief that an overemphasis on precision in scientific research is misguided. They remind us that quantitative indices, while often valuable, should not be pursued solely for their own sake. We identify seven general circumstances where qualitative information greatly enriches research reviews.

1. *Treatments may be individualized.* Quantitative synthesis may be difficult because of treatment flexibility. Some educational and social programs are tailored idiosyncratically

to the person or community receiving them (Yin and Heald, 1975). Such treatment variations do not result from haphazard implementation. Rather, there is an intentional effort to individualize.

An example is Public Law 94-142, passed by Congress in 1975. This law requires that every child with an educational handicap receive special services. It covers many handicaps, including physical, cognitive, and emotional, and so the services provided are extremely diverse and specialized. The desired outcomes vary as much as the treatments. For a child with emotional problems, the treatment might be therapeutic counseling to alleviate severe depression. For a partially deaf child, services might involve supportive aides to improve school performance. A dyslexic child might need special tutoring. A blind child would receive different services.

Quantitative synthesis across studies of children getting different treatments aimed toward different goals is unlikely to produce useful information about overall program success. Asking the question "Is Public Law 94-142 effective?" is rather like asking, "Is HUD effective?" It is an interesting question, but the answer will vary depending upon which HUD program is under discussion (for example, rent subsidies, urban renewal, energy conservation). The same is true of education programs with clearly individualized treatments.

For these efforts, nonquantitative information becomes important in two ways. First, it is necessary to carefully document the *process* aspects of each treatment as well as the outcome. Following this, it may be possible to summarize outcomes across a group of children receiving similar services. Second, developing an *overall* estimate of program effectiveness requires aggregating across dramatically different treatment modalities. It may be that 94-142 has been highly successful in improving the school performance of deaf and dyslexic children, but much less so for blind and emotionally disturbed children. In addition, individual treatments for one subgroup of participants may be particularly expensive relative to other program components. Combining these findings into some sort of statistical average or aggregate using quantitative synthesis would say little about the law's effectiveness; the differences between particular groups of children and treatment modalities might be obscured by an overall statistic. A policymaker must balance the various sources of disparate information when deciding if the law is working well on the whole, or working well in certain ways but not in others.

2. *Critical outcomes may be difficult to measure quantitatively.* An appealing feature of quantitative synthesis is its emphasis on relatively simple numerical indices that are comparable across studies. If the appropriate numerical information is available from several research reports, synthesis can proceed smoothly. Doing this transforms complicated, unclear, or "messy" original research into precise numerical summaries.

But there is a real risk of false precision. We all know that certain outcomes are difficult to capture numerically. The context in which certain programs operate is sometimes far more important than any easily quantifiable narrow, specific feature. Even when test scores or similar measures are used routinely to evaluate certain programs, investigators may legitimately question how appropriate they are under varying circumstances. One example is the perpetual debate over how to interpret scores on standard intelligence tests, despite their popularity in educational evaluations (Zigler and Trickett, 1978).

As Zimiles (1980) points out, this problem becomes particularly tricky in evaluations of complex programs:

Most programs for children, especially educational programs, are aimed at producing a multiplicity of outcomes. As already noted, many of the psychological characteristics they are concerned with fostering—whether it be ego strength, or resourcefulness, or problem solving ability—are difficult or impossible to measure, especially within the time and cost constraints of an evaluation study. The usual response to this dilemma is to shift through the roster of multiple outcomes and single out for assessment, not the most important ones, but those that are capable of being measured (p. 7).

Here an evaluator is faced with a tradeoff between precision and meaning. Organizing a synthesis forces us to confront a similar dilemma. Which outcomes appearing in the studies should be included, or emphasized, in a synthesis? If we decide not to rely exclusively on quantitative measures, we must devise a method for incorporating nonquantitative evidence to strengthen our review.

3. *Assessing program effects across multiple levels of impact.* Quantitative procedures work best when all studies assess program effects at the same level or unit of impact. While this level often is the individual participant, programs can have impact at other levels as well (Yin and Heald, 1975). For example, while most daycare studies focus on the behavior of participating children, the availability of substitute care also influences families and the labor market (Belsky and Steinberg, 1978).

Suppose a program's influence is felt at several levels. Then the need to make an overall decision about it may force the aggregating of results across different levels as well as across outcomes measured at the same level. Synthesis at any particular level can profit from quantitative methods. But the aggregation across several levels usually demands qualitative decisions about tradeoffs.

For example, in the early 1970s the National Institute of Education developed a new program called Experimental Schools (Herriot, 1978). From more than 100 applicants, 10 rural school systems were selected to try various innovations. Money was offered to support these innovations for an initial trial period, with the hope that if the changes were successful they would be institutionalized. There was also hope that other school systems throughout the country, seeing positive results from these 10 Experimental Schools districts, would voluntarily adopt the most successful new ideas.

Outcomes were measured at three levels: changes in students' academic performances, changes in the organization of the school system, and changes in citizens' perceptions of the schools. As one might anticipate, the results were complicated, and uniformity did not exist at any of the three levels. Yet some promising findings emerged, especially in public perceptions of what roles schools should and do play.

Now suppose a superintendent in an eleventh school system wanted to base some school reforms on results from this project. If she began by examining the available evidence, she would face a matrix of findings. For each of the three "impact levels," there is evidence from each of the ten school districts. These results could be synthesized quantitatively across any one impact level. For example, the average program effect on student test performance across the ten schools could be calculated quite easily. However, synthesis within any district would require nonquantitative analysis of trade-offs between levels of impact. For example, judging a program's overall impact on a particular school district might require trading off a positive effect on public support, a negative impact on school organization, and no influence on student performance. Such a synthesis defies simple quantitative aggregation. One superintendent may have a set of weights to apply to the relative values of changes in student performance versus changes in public understanding and support for the schools; another superintendent may have an entirely different set of weights. The point, in summary, is that aggregating the results of multilevel impact studies nearly always will require the introduction of nonquantitative steps.

A general framework for synthesizing results of multilevel impact programs appears in Figure 4.2. Note that quantitative synthesis applies across any one impact level (row), while qualitative integration of outcomes is necessary for assessing overall program impact at a particular location (column).

4. *The uncontrolled treatment group versus the treated control group.* Salter (1980) points out that when several studies compare people who are receiving a treatment to others who are not, subtle differences between similarly la-

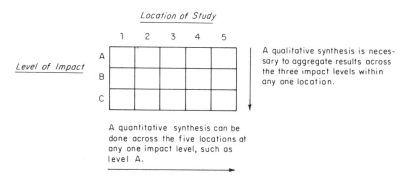

Figure 4.2. Framework for aggregating findings across different levels of impact.

beled treatments are common. Nonquantitative information can offer a reviewer valuable guidance in assessing how similar the treatments really are.

Fosburg and Glantz (1981) provide a recent example. They reviewed a series of studies of children's nutrition programs sponsored by the U.S. Department of Agriculture. The simplest quantitative analysis would have involved computing an effect size for each study, comparing the health of children who received food supplements with those who did not, and then averaging findings across all the studies. But nonquantitative information included in many of the individual studies convinced them this would be fruitless. While for administrative purposes the treatment was the same in each study, information about "plate waste"—food not eaten—of the supplementary food suggested important differences among sites. In some cases plate waste was high; other studies reported almost none. In every case, these data were informal and descriptive. But the reviewers decided this information was crucial. Combining treatments having the same administrative name would in this situation have amounted to combining groups receiving vastly different treatments. They were "uncontrolled."

The same dilemma arose for the control groups. They were not all "pure" control groups, in textbook fashion. Many studies reported that children at sites not receiving assistance from the Department of Agriculture were still getting some food assistance under Title XX of the Social Security Act, which provides various forms of aid to low-income families. So control groups in some of the studies in the review were actually quite heavily "treated," while others were in fact "pure" control groups, receiving no food assistance at all.

In this case, the qualitative description of what actually happened to children in treatment and control groups in each study led the reviewers to reorganize their synthesis into subgroups. These subgroups acknowledged differences between treated versus untreated controls. A simple average of effect sizes over all studies would have missed this step. (Box 4.5 gives another example.)

---

### BOX 4.5.  ARE CONTROL GROUPS COMPARABLE?

A review that aggregates information from studies comparing a treatment group to a control group should offer some reasonable assurance that the various studies are comparing the same things. This means not only that the treatments should be similar across studies but also that the control groups should be comparable. If they are not, it is still possible to combine findings across studies, but a reviewer should be aware of possible differences in outcomes being attributable to differences among control groups. This provides an opportunity for qualitative information to make its contribution.

Close attention was given to controls in Devine and Cook's (1983) review of the effects of psychosocial interventions on length of hospital stay. Devine and Cook present a rigorous quantitative summary of effect sizes from 34 studies of hospitalized patients. They also carefully examine narrative descriptions of how control-group patients were selected, what exact "nontreatment" they received, and whether or not different kinds of control groups seemed to produce systematically different outcomes.

Devine and Cook identify two types of controls: people receiving "usual" hospital care (no psychosocial intervention) and people receiving a "placebo," such as hearing a tape about the preadmission process, hospital facilities, and physical environment. Narrative descriptions suggest that placebo content differs considerably from study to study, with more or less resemblance to the actual psychosocial treatment. Devine and Cook explore this source of variation:

> The variability in placebo content raises the possibility that in some instances the placebo may have been in fact an attenuated form of the treatment . . . A partial test of the influence of different types of placebos on the apparent effectiveness of the experimental treatments can be made by reviewing the three studies which included both placebo and "usual care" control groups. In one of them (Solomon, 1973), the placebo involved a tour of the intensive care unit while the experimental treatment was a psychotherapeutic interview combined with the same tour. The author explicitly noted that the tour, in addition to providing "attention," may also have decreased fears by providing information about what to expect in the hospital. In the second study (David, 1973), the placebo involved several pastoral visits whose effects were contrasted with those of an experimental treatment based on a specific crisis intervention technique. The author noted that patients in the "pastoral visit" placebo group frequently talked about their operations and other matters in a way that could be interpreted as seeking support or help in a crisis. The researcher made no note that such discussion was discouraged. In the third study (Lukas et al., 1976) the placebo was a brief interview with an "interested" psychologist. The researcher noted that conversation was specifically guided away from the operation, recovery, or the future. This was contrasted with the two experimental interventions in the third study which provided information and encouraged realistic future planning for the surgical experience and recovery (p. 427).

This illustrates how descriptive information from individual studies can and should influence the interpretation a reviewer gives to the group as a whole. When a reviewer asks whether control groups are "pure" or "treated," descriptive information from individual studies provides the answer.

---

5. *Studying the "wrong" treatment.* Occasionally when synthesizing outcomes one finds that a relationship between a program and an outcome is not as strong as was originally hoped, but that outcomes are *sometimes* successful. This may lead to a search for features of a program other than the origi-

nal treatment that might explain the success. Here, non-quantitative data can play an important role.

A striking example comes from a recent debate in the field of criminal justice. For many years, rehabilitation of criminal offenders, especially delinquent youths, has been a dearly sought goal of judges, educators, and social workers. Yet, despite large numbers of innovative programs implemented in the last twenty years, evaluations of program effectiveness have generally offered little cause for optimism.

In 1966 Bailey reviewed 100 evaluations and concluded that "evidence supporting the efficacy of correctional treatment is slight, inconsistent, and of questionable reliability" (cited in Wilson, 1980, p. 4.). Hood and Sparks (1970) reviewed a group of European studies with similarly negative findings. But the coup de grace came from a book by Lipton, Martinson, and Wilks (1975). In their review of 231 studies, they found that, "with few and isolated exceptions, the rehabilitative efforts that have been reported so far have had no appreciable effect on recidivism" (cited in Sechrest, White, and Brown, 1979, p. 27).

This widely circulated book threw a wet blanket over the optimism of rehabilitation researchers and practitioners. Yet a study by Murray and Cox (1979) should spark some optimism. They report on 266 youths, classified as serious delinquents, who instead of going to state reformatories were sent to a community-based program called Unified Delinquency Intervention Services. While a quantitative analysis found that the rehabilitation treatment itself was not especially successful for these offenders, Murray and Cox reported that another feature of the program, the degree of supervision of the youths, seemed to be highly related to later arrest rates. This finding was not based on an analysis formally built into the original experimental design, but rather on a qualitative observation that a treatment component not originally planned as part of the rehabilitative process seems to be crucial in determining program outcomes (rearrests). Wilson (1980) gives a good summary of this point:

Youths left in their homes or sent to wilderness camps showed the least reduction [in recidivism]; those placed in group homes in the community showed a greater reduction; and those put into out of town group homes, intensive care residential programs, or sent to regular reformatories showed the greatest reduction. If this is true, it implies [that] how strictly the youths were supervised, rather than what therapeutic programs were available, had the greatest effect on the recidivism rate.

To summarize, a quantitative analysis can systematically examine the relationship between planned program and outcome variables across many studies. But descriptive information from one or several studies can provide clues that a different feature of the treatment, *not formally built into a study's experimental design,* may be more important than the original planned treatment. Murray and Cox found this, and new calls have been made for a closer look at the importance of type of supervision, rather than type of therapeutic program, in determining the success of rehabilitation programs for delinquent youths.

6. *Nonquantitative information can influence policy.* One impetus for developing quantitative methods of synthesis was a wish to make research findings more useful for policy: "If what an integrative analysis shows cannot be stated in one uncomplicated sentence, then its message will be lost on all but a few specialists" (Glass, 1978, p. 3). When presented with a simple numerical summary of the average effect of psychotherapy (Smith and Glass, 1977), or heart bypass graft surgery (Wortman and Yeaton, 1983), or class size (Glass and Smith, 1979), a policymaker can evaluate program effects without wading through volumes of research reports or vague rhetoric.

What format for presenting research findings is "best" remains an open and complicated question. But there are cases where qualitative findings have had a clear policy impact. One such example comes from a General Accounting Office review of cost estimates for long term health care (U.S. General Accounting Office, 1982c). A congressional committee asked the GAO to examine what has been learned about the relative costs of home care versus institutional care for the elderly. Existing legislation reimbursed people only for expenses in nursing homes and other institutions. The goal was to learn if long-term care could be provided at a more reasonable cost if people were reimbursed for home-care expenses. The committee's hypothesis was that home care would be both less expensive and more satisfactory, and therefore that reimbursement would make sense.

The GAO collected two kinds of evidence. Numerical information on costs was indeed clear—home care is nearly always cheaper than institutional care. But qualitative findings from many studies using interviews with the elderly consistently cut in the other direction. They turned up the unexpected idea that many elderly persons who now get *neither* home care nor institutional care, and indeed according to physicians do not seriously need such care, would request it and use substantial resources if home care were reimbursed. The GAO concluded that overall, given limited total resources for health services, offering reimbursement for home care would actually decrease the quality of services for those individuals who need them most, and at the same time would raise the cost for everyone. While these findings were exactly the opposite of what the congressional committee expected, the qualitative reports were so convincing that the move to reimburse home care was dropped.

7. *Qualitative analysis can structure "next steps."* Narrative presentation may be especially useful when the purpose of the review is not to summarize outcomes but rather to stimulate improvements in research or in programs. Reviews often explore questions such as: How are studies designed? What are their major strengths and weaknesses? How easy or difficult was it to implement the treatment? Have any important program characteristics been overlooked? Answering such questions gives newcomers to a field and nonspecialists a broad picture of what the issues are. It gives policymakers some ideas about the strengths and weaknesses of overall

findings and how confident one can be in adopting some of the suggestions. It may offer researchers important insights, not only about how to interpret the findings of existing studies but also about how to improve future efforts.

An example of using a narrative review to improve research comes from the response of criminal justice professionals to the review by Lipton, Martinson, and Wilks (1975) of 231 studies of rehabilitation of delinquents. The authors' finding, mentioned earlier, is that "with few and isolated instances, the rehabilitative efforts that have been reported so far have had no appreciable effect on recidivism" (Sechrest, White, and Brown, 1979, p. 27). This detailed summary had such a sharp impact on both academic researchers and corrections administrators that in 1976 the National Academy of Sciences convened a blue-ribbon panel of experts. Its charge was to "review existing evaluations to determine whether they provide a basis for any conclusions about the effectiveness of rehabilitative techniques, clarifying the difficulties of measuring the effectiveness of treatment programs, and recommending methodological strategies for evaluating treatment programs" (Sechrest, White, and Brown, 1979, p. 4).

The panel included specialists in corrections, economists, lawyers, statisticians, psychologists, sociologists, and administrators. They represented diverse political perspectives. Using the Lipton, Martinson, and Wilks narrative review as a takeoff point, they looked carefully at existing rehabilitation research and found many weaknesses, including poor research designs, ineffective measurement of outcomes, and incompletely or poorly implemented treatments. A subsample of those studies were selected by Fienberg and Grambsch (1979) for reevaluation and reanalysis. They found that "where the original review erred, it was almost invariably by an overly lenient assessment of the methodology of a study or by a failure to maintain an appropriately critical set in evaluating statistical analyses. The net result was that Lipton et al. were, if anything, more likely to accept evidence in favor of rehabilitation than was justified" (p. 119).

Three consequences follow from this National Academy review. First, researchers and administrators now have a context in which to place past research. Second, future research on the rehabilitation of delinquents should be strengthened by the specific suggestions of Sechrest, White, and Brown (1979). Finally, new substantive suggestions emerged from the review itself. For example, one recommendation is that more attention be paid to the needs of and opportunities for rehabilitative programs outside prisons. Descriptive information in evaluations often indicated that prison is an ineffective place for many interventions, such as job training and counseling. The review also found scattered evidence that the timing of certain types of interventions is critical, suggesting that research on timing might be particularly productive.

To summarize, a narrative review led to a better understanding of weaknesses in existing studies. It generated specific suggestions for promising innovations in the future. It also offered a context for scattered findings, incorporating details about program implementations and study designs as well as outcomes. While a quantitative synthesis might have simplified the structure of the outcome summaries, the goal of improving research was well served by the discursive format. (See Box 4.6 for another example.)

---

**BOX 4.6.  SUPPLEMENTING REVIEWS WITH QUALITATIVE INFORMATION FROM INDIVIDUAL STUDIES**

One important role for case reports or narrative information is to supplement numerical and quantitative data. An example comes from the National Academy of Sciences' report examining how mentally retarded children are placed in special settings. Shonkoff (1982) reviewed the literature on how retarded children are categorized before placement. He found many research reports giving incidences of different categories of retardation or special needs, but before doing a simple quantitative summary he notes a major caution:

The bulk of the epidemiological literature does not conform to the American Association of Mental Deficiency (AAMD) requirement that a diagnosis of mental retardation be based on well standardized measurement of both adaptive and intellectual deficits. Smith and Polloway, for example, found the inclusion of adaptive behavior measures in less than 10 percent of the recent research efforts that they reviewed. Cleland (1979) reported that many studies mismatched individuals' test scores with the appropriate level of retardation. In an analysis of 566 articles in the *American Journal of Mental Deficiency and Retardation* from 1973 to 1979, Taylor (1980) found that only 28 percent included terminology consistent with the AAMD classifications, confirming Cleland's assertions by demonstrating that almost 20 percent of the studies he reviewed included subjects who had been inappropriately classified based on data presented in the article itself. Interpretation of such information clearly presents major problems.

This detailed "digging in" to discover what processes underlie numerical results or categorizations identified misclassification as a serious problem. No quantitative analysis of placements by itself would turn up the troubling finding that children were being misclassified according to AAMD standards.

## Allying Statistical and Descriptive Evidence

We have argued that nonquantitative information can vastly enrich scientific literature reviews. The ultimate goal is to enhance the *interaction* between numerical and qualitative evidence. We now present three specific illustrations of their complementary roles in research synthesis. These three examples show how the advantages of combining numbers and narrative far outweigh the simplicity offered by an exclusive choice between paradigms.

1. *Using statistics to identify relationships that are not apparent from visual inspection.* One view of formal quantitative methods is *adversarial*. Statistical significance is a dreaded hurdle that must be cleared before a study is considered legitimate and worthy of discussion. This view is

especially common among graduate students working on dissertations and researchers hoping to publish their work. Because of the relationship between statistical significance and sample size, encouraging findings may be discarded simply because they come from studies with small samples and therefore fail to reach an acceptable level of significance.

Some recent comparisons of statistical and visual criteria for assessing change suggest that statistics are more often ally than adversary. By relying solely on visual inspection of data summaries and subjective judgment, we sometimes overlook small but reliable effects. One example is the work of Jones, Weinrott, and Vaught (1978) involving the results of operant experiments. They had university faculty, researchers, and graduate students visually inspect a series of graphs and judge whether or not a reliable change had occurred. The changes also were examined statistically using standard time-series analyses. Comparison of visual and statistical procedures indicated that the latter were more sensitive, leading to the following conclusion: "If time-series analysis were used to supplement visual analysis ... researchers probably would infer meaningful changes in their data more often than if visual inferences alone were used to analyze operant experiments" (p. 280).

A second example is Szucko and Kleinmuntz's (1981) comparison of clinical versus statistical procedures for detecting lies from polygraph charts. Six experienced polygraph interpreters who conducted "intuitive" evaluations were pitted against statistical procedures. The results demonstrated clear advantages of statistical detection: "Our results strongly suggest that human judges are ill-equipped to interpret polygraph protocols ... What we are suggesting based on our findings, therefore, is that the formula is better than the head and that lie detector tests should be interpreted actuarially rather than intuitively" (pp. 494–495). These examples are consistent with most studies comparing statistical and clinical procedures: statistics usually are more sensitive to small effects within a single study (Kratochwill, 1977; Meehl, 1965).

Can these findings be generalized to methods of combining studies as well? Apparently so. Cooper and Rosenthal (1980) had university faculty and graduate students summarize the results of seven investigations of sex differences in task persistence. Half of the reviewers were asked to "employ whatever criteria you would use if this exercise were being undertaken for a class term paper or a manuscript for publication" (p. 445), while the other half were taught statistical combinatorial procedures. While several of the individual studies did not show significant sex differences, statistical aggregation demonstrated an overall significant effect favoring females ($p = .016$).

Descriptive reviewers were significantly more likely than statistical reviewers to find little or no support for the hypothesis of a sex difference in persistence. "Traditional reviewers either neglect probabilities or combine them intuitively in an overly conservative fashion" (p. 448). However, statistical reviewers did not unquestioningly accept the hypothesis as "proven." No one in either group concluded that there "definitely" was support for the hypothesis. In addition, the type of reviewing procedure was not strongly related to recommendations for future research, or to judgments about the methodological adequacy of studies. Statistical reviewers cautiously interpreted rather than blindly accepted numerical indices.

These findings suggest that statistical procedures can help a reviewer to identify relationships that may not be large enough to detect informally. The worth of these procedures should increase as the number of studies grows large, or when a program effect is small. One might wonder why a reviewer should be excited about turning up positive but small effects. We can suggest two reasons. First, the limits on the degree of control that can be exerted over program participants in educational or medical innovations are likely to lead to small or incremental gains rather than "slam-bang" effects (Gilbert, Light, and Mosteller, 1975; Gilbert, McPeek, and Mosteller, 1977; Gottman and Glass, 1978). To wait for a new curriculum that doubles reading scores may be to wait forever. Second, when a small effect is detected, it sometimes can be enhanced by refinements in the program. This requires a judgment about whether a modest finding is worth pursuing. Process analysis and expert judgment become particularly important here. This brings us to suggest a way to ally descriptive evidence with quantitative findings.

2. *Using nonquantitative evidence after detecting a program effect.* Statistical procedures can help both to identify small effects and to formalize the search for unusually successful or unsuccessful program outcomes, or "outliers." But such findings, standing alone, are not very informative (Klitgaard, 1978). Suppose a reviewer looking at a dozen evaluations finds that, on the average, curriculum A slightly outperforms B, or that a review of ten studies of urban high schools shows one to be unusually effective. What is one to make of these results? Formal procedures can *detect* subtle differences, but they cannot *explain* them. They offer a starting point, not a final answer.

After an effect is identified statistically, the reviewer must try to explain why this finding exists. Is it replicable? What program characteristics are responsible? Can it be enlarged or improved? Answering these questions requires further efforts that often rely heavily on case studies and descriptive evidence. For example, McClintock, Brannon, and Maynard-Moody (1979) discuss Lazar and Darlington's (1978) quantitative synthesis of a group of preschool programs:

Had each of the original investigations been a qualitative case study, then merging the data and collecting similar data at a later point in time would have been impossible. On the other hand, the absence of rich qualitative descriptions of the organizational features of the intervention programs made it difficult to explain some of the anomalies of the quantitative analyses. This suggests that research on single cases that incorporates a combination of qualitative and quantitative approaches would be optimal for secondary analysis and direct comparison with other cases (p. 624).

Here, qualitative information is deemed necessary to explain the quantitative findings. We believe this example illustrates a more general point: qualitative case descriptions are particularly valuable in helping program managers to *interpret* statistical findings. Most managers are conscientious and want to strengthen their programs as much as possible. For them, it is especially useful to have descriptive data such as: What are the characteristics of successful implementations? How were the teachers trained? How were parents involved? What were details of the educational program? This information helps a manager to improve a program incrementally, using comparative findings from a review that gives insights about *why* certain versions of a program or curriculum work better than others. It can also point out limitations of quantitative evidence (see Box 4.7).

Descriptive information can help a manager make decisions at a micro program level, and at the same time it can inform macro decisions about program effectiveness, sometimes across hundreds of local sites. An illustration of this important function comes from federal regulation of daycare. Anticipating that the Federal Interagency Day Care Requirements would soon come up for renewal, in 1975 the Department of Health, Education and Welfare commissioned a four-year study of how different features of daycare centers affect participating children (Ruopp et al., 1979). Existing studies were reviewed, and new quantitative studies were conducted at 57 sites. These included eight randomized trials and 49 "natural" experiments. The investigators expected two main policy variables to influence children: staff-to-child ratio (the higher the better), and level of staff training (the more the better). Group size, a third feature of the daycare centers, though not originally expected to be particularly important, turned out in the quantitative analysis across sites to be the most critical feature. Children in very large groups performed less well than children in smaller groups. This finding appeared in the quantitative analyses of both the randomized experiments and the "natural" studies.

To explain this unexpected result, careful process studies were done. They were qualitative and narrative in form. These analyses across many sites helped to explain why a center with 4 staff members and 32 children had poorer outcomes on the average than a center with 2 staff members and 16 children, even though both had identical staff-to-child

---

**BOX 4.7. NARRATIVE INFORMATION CAN QUALIFY SEEMINGLY CONSISTENT FINDINGS**

When many studies reach a similar statistical conclusion, it is tempting to believe that, on balance, this conclusion is correct. But descriptive information can throw some doubt upon the common finding. This happened in Shadish's (1982) excellent review of research on the effectiveness of preventive health care for children.

Shadish looked at 38 controlled empirical studies, which as a group offered strong evidence *from the words in the conclusions* that preventive health care for children was valuable. Interventions targeted to specific problems had the most support, while the value of broad-scale programs was less clear.

When analyzing narrative descriptions of studies, Shadish found serious validity problems. For example, many studies had high attrition rates of participating families: in one study 50 percent dropped out, in another, 80 percent of the original participants did not return for reinterview. In addition, the overwhelming majority of studies failed to assess or to report on the implementation of the treatments. This leads to two problems. First, "with some broadly defined treatments such as comprehensive care, little knowledge is available to suggest exactly what activities were conducted under the treatment. Lacking this knowledge, it is hard to replicate the results, or to know exactly what aspect of the treatment was responsible for what effects" (p. 45). Second, "it is not possible to know if a given treatment produced poor results because it doesn't work, or because it was not administered" (p. 45). More information is necessary.

Shadish concludes that while we have reason to be optimistic about the value of preventive health care for children, the overall quality of evidence about effectiveness is not strong enough to assert that "we know it works."

ratios of 1:8. Four adults in a room together spend a large fraction of their time talking to one another rather than focusing on the children. Also, with several staff members present, any one adult can assume, sometimes incorrectly, that "everyone else" is watching the children.

The quantitative analyses, together with the qualitative investigation of underlying reasons, were presented in 1979. They highlighted the unexpected importance of group size, and argued that regulators should focus on this feature, as well as on staff-to-child ratio and staff education, in federally subsidized daycare centers. New Federal Interagency Day Care Requirements were published in 1980. They drew heavily on both the numerical and the narrative summaries, and a central feature was a limitation on group size (Boruch and Cordray, 1981).

3. *Using the alliance to capitalize on conflicting outcomes.* We have emphasized the value of using quantitative and descriptive studies as allies rather than adversaries for synthesizing data. Some years ago a review of the two different kinds of studies led to a set of complex findings, yet we believe this example illustrates our argument. As we mentioned in Chapter 2, a group of educators and psychologists working with mentally retarded individuals in the 1940s came to believe that glutamic acid would improve a person's capacity to learn, and that this would be reflected by higher IQ scores. A series of uncontrolled studies and case reports appeared in the medical and psychological literatures, most of them finding a modest improvement in the IQ's of retarded people receiving the drug.

These findings did not go unchallenged. Skeptics pointed out many threats to the validity of the studies and questioned how the drug worked physiologically to improve IQ. A series of controlled clinical trials were carried out as a follow-up to examine the effects of glutamic acid more systematically. For example, McCulloch (1950) used matched experimental and control groups, with controls receiving a placebo. Caretakers and examiners were not informed of subjects' group membership. Several of these experiments showed quickly and convincingly that glutamic acid did not outperform the placebo, though both groups showed an improvement over people receiving only the usual custodial care common in the 1940s. Astin and Ross (1960) summarized the discrepant findings between case reports and experimental studies, and concluded that the experimental evidence was far more convincing: glutamic acid is ineffective.

It is tempting to conclude from this example that the controlled, experimental, quantitative studies were right, while the uncontrolled studies were wrong, and that the latter served no useful scientific purpose. We come to a somewhat different conclusion: the conflicting results from *all* the studies carry valuable information about improving the lives of retarded individuals. The controlled experiments are indeed convincing that glutamic acid does not raise IQ. But something was still working on the patients' behalf, since most of the earlier case reports documented gains in IQ. Scientists were pressed to account for the improvement.

Contrasting the controlled and uncontrolled studies prompts us to examine the context in which the drug was administered. Including the uncontrolled studies in our review reveals an example of "studying the wrong treatment," discussed earlier. People receiving glutamic acid got far more environmental stimulation than was typical for people receiving the usual custodial care. This extra attention and increased expectations also seemed to improve the performance of the placebo group in the experimental trials. One study (Zabrenko and Chambers, 1952) focused on this environmental stimulation hypothesis directly and confirmed its positive impact on IQ.

This example illustrates how different forms of evidence, taken together, can lead to insights with important policy implications. The seemingly inconsistent findings end up providing information about *both* glutamic acid and supportive environments. Conflicts in outcomes have not hindered us. They have enriched practice.

The controversy over glutamic acid occurred more than a generation ago, but the lesson still applies today. Different types of evidence are complementary, and singlemindedness about either quantitative or qualitative approaches to synthesis imposes unnecessary limits on what we can learn from the work of others. The pursuit of good science should transcend personal preferences for numbers or narrative.

# 5

Our fundamental assumption in this book is that society needs to understand better what individual studies have found. Research summaries can organize findings in a powerful way. We firmly believe this, and we expect that as reviews improve they will advance knowledge in many fields. Even now, some reviews have strengthened both science and policy. While the results are not carved in stone, they have illuminated substantive questions, resolved conflicts, and contributed methodological insights. They have helped society to discover what is already known.

## Reviews Have Cemented Substantive Findings

Well-done reviews can identify general trends that are unlikely to emerge in any single study, however broad or well designed.

### Coronary Artery Bypass Surgery

More than 100,000 people have coronary bypass graft surgery in America each year. Wortman and Yeaton (1983) examine 20 studies comparing bypass surgery to drug treatment. They explore the view that surgery is preferable. Detailed results among the 20 studies differ considerably. But the bulk of the evidence shows that surgery works better than drug treatment. Wortman and Yeaton also look separately at patients with different levels of heart disease, and conclude that patients with three-vessel disease benefit especially from surgery.

A feature that strengthens Wortman and Yeaton's review is their effort to adjust results of different studies because of methodological differences. As we discuss in Chapter 3, attention to variations in the research process can modify substantive findings. For example, sometimes patients who were receiving drugs and did not improve were switched out of the drug treatment and into surgery. When this happened, the original investigators usually counted these crossovers as completing treatment in the drug group, so they would not "contaminate" the surgical group with self-selection. Wortman and Yeaton examined the relationship between crossover rates and the comparative effectiveness of the two treatments. The smaller the crossover rate, the greater the benefits of surgery. Crossovers apparently reduced the number of drug group patients who might otherwise have died. Taking this research finding into account enhances the advantage of surgery over drugs. This insight was identified by looking across studies with different crossover rates; it could not appear in any single study.

### Class Size

Glass and Smith (1979) summarize 77 studies relating class size to student achievement. The cost implications are substantial. If class size does not matter much, school districts could increase the student-to-teacher ratio and reduce costs per student dramatically.

While expert opinion about the impact of class size on learning has been split for decades, Glass and Smith's review turned up clear results. Class size matters, although not an enormous amount. Students in very small classes (say, 10 students or fewer) do noticeably better than similar students in average-sized classes (say, 20 students). Students in large classes (say, 30 or more) do slightly worse than similar students in average-sized classes. This relationship is strongest for the subset of well-controlled studies, where students were randomly assigned to classes of different sizes. Glass and Smith look at whether special features of the classes seem to strengthen or weaken these findings. Their statistical analyses show a slightly stronger relationship for high school than for elementary school. But findings do not differ appreciably across different academic subjects, levels of student IQ, or any other demographic feature of classrooms.

Two points about this review are especially interesting. First, the relationship between class size and student performance is modest. Therefore, because of small samples, many individual studies did not turn up statistically significant differences. Statistical reviewing procedures were necessary to identify the advantage of smaller classes. Second, a policy payoff of research on class size comes from seeing if *changing* class size will matter. Therefore, finding that controlled studies using random assignment of students to classes turned up a clear relation between class size and performance nailed down the conclusion. Once again, a review was able to detect a modest relationship often missed by individual studies.

### Innovative Reading Programs

Pflaum, Walberg, Karegianes, and Rasher (1980) examine 97 studies comparing different ways of teaching young children to read. Researchers in this area have looked at many instructional methods. The reviewers set as one goal pinning down which teaching method was, on average, best.

They found that several methods for teaching worked about equally well, with one program ("sound-symbol blending") showing special promise. But they discovered an additional result with far broader policy implications. It is that regardless of the detailed curriculum, innovative methods and new experimental programs substantially outperform any standard curriculum, whatever the standard is: "Specially designed instruction generally tends to produce more learning than less systematic instruction, assuming that control treatments may be less well thought out or operationalized compared with experimental treatments" (pp. 17–18).

These findings have clear value for policy. They indicate that the type of reading curriculum is less important than the overall organizational attention given to teaching reading. This suggests that policymakers who wish to strengthen literacy could profitably focus on administrative direction in schools rather than on curricular details.

## Reviews Help to Interpret Other Findings

Some reviews give general insight into interpreting research studies.

### Pretests

Willson and Putnam (1982) investigate what happens when a research study includes a formal pretest prior to intervention as well as a posttest afterwards. They look at 32 studies comparing posttest scores of pretested and nonpretested groups. One motivating question is whether simply taking a first test improves scores on a second. If it does, then researchers must take special care to disentangle program effects from pretest effects.

A second issue is substantive. If pretests consistently raise test scores, this buttresses an argument of critics of standardized testing. Critics contend that familiarity with test taking in general can substantially improve performance. In other words, they argue that a test assesses experience as well as ability.

Willson and Putnam reach two conclusions. One supports the critics of standardized tests while the other weakens their case. First, the review shows that pretests indeed raise people's scores on posttests. Individuals taking any exam generally do slightly better on a follow-up exam. But the second finding is that the duration of time between the two tests matters. For exams given within a month after a pretest, the pretest appears to raise the later exam's scores. But after about a month this improvement erodes dramatically. This runs counter to the argument that people with prior exposure have a clear advantage.

### Gender and Cognitive Abilities

Rosenthal and Rubin's (1982c) review of gender differences in cognitive abilities reports that males generally outperform females in quantitative, spatial, and articulation performance, while females generally do better on tests of verbal abilities.

Such findings normally lead to debate about whether the differences are mainly genetic or mainly environmental. Rosenthal and Rubin approach this issue with a new empirical slant. They check whether the date of publication of a study is related to the size of reported sex differences. It turns out that, in all four areas, females gain in cognitive performance relative to males as time passes. Rosenthal and Rubin conclude: "Of course we cannot say whether this marked linear trend for females to gain relative to males in cognitive skills is due to changes in the nature of the studies over the years. But we can say that whatever the reason, in these studies females appear to be gaining in cognitive skill relative to males rather faster than the gene can travel!" (p. 211). Interestingly, Hall's (1978) review of nonverbal decoding skills also found that women improved relative to men over time. Using a review to investigate historical changes in outcomes has given new insight that no "one moment in time" study can provide.

## Reviews Can Resolve Controversies

Because reviews use each study as a unit of analysis, they can systematically examine the impact of different research designs or different treatment formats. This can sometimes help to resolve apparent conflicts in a research literature.

### Block Grants versus Categorical Programs

Since the late 1970s there has been continuing debate in Congress over how best to allocate money, and the services that money buys, to poor people. Two prominent mechanisms are categorical programs and block grants. With categorical programs, control over the money and the details of distribution remains in federal hands. In contrast, block grants distribute funds to a general-purpose governmental unit, such as a state, city, or municipality, for broad use in broad areas.

In 1982 the Subcommittee on Oversight of the Ways and Means Committee of the U.S. House of Representatives asked the General Accounting Office to compare block grants to categorical aid. There had been no systematic summing up of research evidence until this effort. Advocates of block grants argued that targeting assistance and services to poor people would be enhanced by more local discretion. Advocacy groups for the poor generally disagreed with that argument, and expected the opposite (Ad Hoc Coalition, 1981).

To resolve this controversy the GAO synthesized the findings of eight studies spanning the decade 1970–1980. The studies' sources vary widely, including the Brookings Institution, academic economists, the National Commission for Employment Policy, and several different government agencies. The GAO report found no differences in how well the two distribution procedures targeted assistance to poor people.

This was true of several different programs, including CETA (job training), CDBG (community development projects), and Title 20 programs (social services). Following the GAO review, debate continues about what is the best way to distribute funds to the poor. But the debate now focuses more clearly on the political aspects of different preferences. No longer does each side argue that *research evidence* shows clearly that its way is better. Block grants versus categorical aid may remain a controversy, but at least the terms of argument are now staked out more clearly.

### Coaching for SAT Exams

Many nervous college applicants preparing to take the Scholastic Aptitude Test (SAT) think seriously about obtaining special coaching or tutoring. Newspapers in cities throughout America advertise such courses. Critics often question their value, especially in light of the claim that the SAT assesses "aptitude" rather than "achievement." The furor grew loud enough during President Carter's administration that the Federal Trade Commission conducted hearings to assess the effects of coaching. The findings showed coaching to have "questionable" value. In contrast, a review by Slack and Porter (1980) found that coaching can raise scores substantially, and so the debate continued.

DerSimonian and Laird (1983) review 19 studies of coaching for the SAT Verbal subtest, and 17 studies for the SAT Math subtest. They especially look at the question we discuss in Chapters 3 and 4: whether the various studies of coaching estimate a single underlying treatment value. They also take into account the impact of using different research designs. We quote from their findings:

Our analysis . . . shows on average a positive gain but also a large variation in the effect of coaching from study to study that cannot be explained by sampling error. A large part of this variation can be explained by the method of evaluation. When coached students are simply compared to national norms, as in uncontrolled studies, the mean gains in verbal and math scores are about 40 to 50 points. For controlled, but unmatched and unrandomized studies, the mean gain is about 15 points for both math and verbal scores, and is reduced to about 10 points for matched and randomized studies. (p. 13).

These findings are interesting for several reasons. First, they illustrate the strong effect of research design on studies of the value of coaching. Second, they demonstrate how a review can detect this interesting result—that outcomes vary depending upon design—while no single study could. But most important, the review pins down convincingly the "best" estimate of coaching. It is about 10 points. On average, coaching is indeed worth something. The 10-point gain is statistically significant. Yet potential customers should be clear that coaching is not usually worth a lot. Applicants must decide for themselves whether an expected real gain of about 10 points is worth the time and expense of a coaching school. But now at least the choice is more clearly laid out.

### Preventive Health Care for Children

Shadish (1982) examined 38 studies of preventive health care for children. Most parents able to afford such care routinely seek it out. They bring their very young children to see a pediatrician several times a year for checkups. Even with older children a visit once a year is widely accepted. Clearly the goal of such regular visits is preventive care in the broadest sense. The pediatrician gets to know the child and family, checks for benchmarks of normal development, and keeps an eye out for any early troubling signs or warning signals.

Many parents accept the value of such regular visits. But some in the health community are questioning them. Just as the annual checkup for adults is no longer unanimously considered a sensible idea, public health researchers and policymakers are uncertain of the value of "well baby care." For example, contrast the conclusion, "Children need continuing and comprehensive medical attention aimed at prevention" (Harvard Child Health Project, 1977), with "Pediatric care has little impact on children's health" (Ghez and Grossman, 1979).

Shadish undertook his review to see which of these opposite views was more congruent with empirical evidence. The findings surprised him and many others. His bottom line was that the methodological inadequacies in nearly all of the studies are so severe that *no firm conclusion* in either direction is justified: "In view of the evidence, then, neither strong advocacy of nor strong opposition to preventive child health care seems warranted" (p. 48). Shadish argues convincingly that while *any* study can be faulted for being imperfect, the drawbacks of studies in this area are so pervasive that no final decision about the value of preventive care is possible. He warns us not to discard existing evidence; there is "somewhat encouraging" support for prevention, but it simply is not solid enough to be conclusive. His review does not resolve the controversy over the value of preventive health care for children. But it shows that a few well-designed evaluations might win a lot for the public.

### Deinstitutionalization in Mental Health

A fourth example of how a research review can illuminate a controversy is Straw's (1983) summary of 30 studies examining alternatives to hospitalization for mentally ill patients. The patients suffered from mental problems that had required hospitalization in the immediate past, or that in the opinion of experts would require it in the near future. Alternative treatments varied, including home care with foster families, outpatient status in mental health facilities, and halfway houses.

The issue of alternatives to hospitalization involves both social values and money. Before the 1950s most publicly supported psychiatric services were offered at state hospitals.

Since then, there has been substantial movement away from hospitalization where possible, toward outpatient and community-based services. While many mental health specialists regard this movement as constructive, there remains an undercurrent of worry about whether services outside of hospitals and other specialized institutions are genuinely meeting the needs of the mentally ill (Mollica, 1983).

Straw's review turns up findings that should reassure proponents of deinstitutionalization. He does not find that alternatives to hospitalization do significantly better. But he does find that these alternatives *are no worse,* and that they cost less than inpatient treatment. And there is scattered evidence of additional value to nonhospitalization. For example, significantly fewer patients in the community-mental-health-center samples than in the state-hospital samples were subsequently hospitalized. Straw's findings dovetail with the judgment of courts that have to assign mentally ill people somewhere. Courts have argued that each person should be put in the "least restrictive environment" that is feasible. Straw demonstrates that, on empirical as well as legal grounds, this makes sense and should continue.

## Reviews Can Teach Broad Lessons about Accumulating Evidence

An increasing number of research reviews use systematic procedures of the sorts we discuss in Chapter 3. It is therefore possible to stand back and reflect on their contributions more broadly. In addition to specific findings, they offer some general insights about what researchers and policymakers should expect to find as evidence accumulates in diverse areas of inquiry. We present three such lessons.

### Most Evaluations Find Small Effects

This is not an extraordinary finding. Earlier work (Gilbert, Light, and Mosteller, 1975) reports a similar result. Review after review confirms it and drives it home. Its importance comes from having managers understand that they should not expect large, positive findings to emerge routinely from a single study of a new program. Indeed, *any* positive findings are good news. This is not a political idea, but rather a statistical one. There are several reasons why, even when an innovation works, an evaluation may underestimate or overlook it.

One possible explanation is low statistical power. Study sample sizes may not be large enough to detect a program effect even if it really exists. A second is unreliability of measurement. If both a program's features and its outcomes are measured with error, then the chance of detecting small effects can drop dramatically. A third explanation is that with multisite innovations only some sites really will experience the positive effects. With new programs in particular, it would be extraordinary if *all* sites, and all program variants, worked equally well. If it were so easy to mount new programs to solve social, educational, and health problems that have persisted over many years, we would live in an engineer's ideal world. The more likely reality is that new programs (whether CETA, Head Start, or a new hospital emergency room procedure) differ from place to place in their implementation, work well in some places, and add little in others. Evaluating outcomes at a few sites may lead to just one or two clear successes, while other sites may show nothing special.

Usual standards for judging program effects also have contributed to pessimism about how well social innovations are doing. Often such standards seem overly conservative. For example, the Coleman Report (1966) estimated that, after taking into account family background, the strength of the relationship between level of school resources and student achievement is modest: $R^2$ is only about .10. Most educators at the time were deeply disappointed with this finding. Yet disappointment that school resources explain "only" 10 percent of the variation in achievement seems unwarranted.

Rosenthal and Rubin's work presented in Chapter 3 (see

Box 3.4) makes a real contribution here. Recall that they reformulate the standard correlation coefficient into a comparison between two proportions. This is easily displayed in a simple two-by-two contingency table. The display gives non-statisticians (and many statisticians also) a much better feel for the practical meaning of an average correlation. For example, we find that an $R^2$ of .10, rarely large enough to create tremendous excitement in evaluation circles, is equivalent to a new treatment's cutting a failure rate, or death rate, or dropout rate by one-half (from 66 percent to 33 percent). This is well worth noticing! Such analogies are useful. They put the Coleman finding into a different light. In future research reviews, small average correlations will command new respect, at least from us.

### Research Design Matters

Many syntheses drive home a point that research methodologists often speculate about: research design matters. One example is the review by DerSimonian and Laird (1983), discussed earlier. They conclude that coaching for SAT exams helps a lot, a modest amount, or hardly at all, depending primarily on the research design of the evaluation. Observational studies generally find that coaching really helps; matched designs turn up a smaller positive value; randomized designs find coaching to be only slightly effective. A second example is Wortman and Yeaton's (1983) review of heart bypass surgery. When examined with observational research designs, surgery appears far more effective than drug treatment. This advantage shrinks noticeably when comparisons are made between randomly assigned groups.

Should one conclude from these two examples that randomized trials always lead to smaller estimates of effects? This idea would be broadly consistent with the discussion by Hoaglin and colleagues (1982), who cite a research review by Chalmers (1982) of portacaval shunt surgery. Chalmers found a strong negative relationship between the degree of experimental control and how well the surgery fared. Controls were adequate in 7 evalutions: *none* of the 7 report high enthusiasm for the surgery. Out of 67 studies where controls were absent, 50 authors were highly enthusiastic. This is in accord with Hugo Muench's tongue-in-cheek rule, "Results can always be improved by omitting controls" (from Bearman, Loewenson, and Gullen, 1974).

Yet some reviews suggest that this rule is not universal. For example, Stock and colleagues (1983) find no relationship between research design and outcomes in studies of age and mental well-being. Similarly, Straw (1983) finds no relationship in his review of effects of deinstitutionalization in mental health. Finally, in a thorough review of innovations in urban government, Yin and Yates (1974) find the *opposite* relationship. They report that the better-controlled research designs tended to find innovations *more* effective. They suggest as an explanation that individuals who are well trained and competent enough to evaluate their efforts with a strong research design also are more likely than average to have developed a thoughtful innovation, which in turn is more likely to be successful.

The point here is not that an overall rule exists. Rather, it is that many reviews find a clear relationship between research design and outcomes (see Box 5.1). Whatever the field, an effort should be made to examine this possibility. Finding such a relationship can then enrich readers' interpretations of results from any one particular study.

### Good Reviews Examine Interactions

It is tempting to focus a review entirely on the first broad question we suggest in Chapter 2, "Does the treatment work?" Many early reviews tried to answer *only* this question, and ignored entirely the more complex ones we also suggest: "For whom does the treatment work best?" and

"Under what circumstances does the treatment work best?" Exemplary reviews that take these extra steps have two virtues. First, the reviews simply demonstrate that interactions can be identified. Second, the answers they turn up are con-

---

**BOX 5.1.  RESEARCH DESIGN CAN INFLUENCE FINDINGS**

Glass and Smith's (1979) review of research on class size dramatically illustrates the impact of study design on findings. Figure B shows the relationship between class size and student achievement for well-controlled and poorly controlled studies. Well-controlled studies used random assignment of students to classes. The effect of class size is striking in controlled studies, but far less so in uncontrolled studies. A review that overlooked research design would underestimate the influence of class size on student performance.

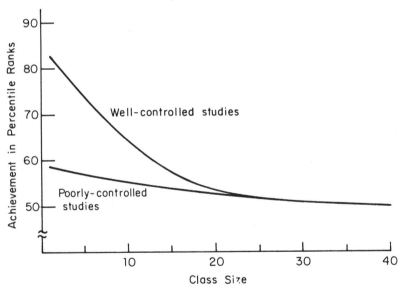

Figure B. Consistent regression lines for the regression of achievement (expressed in percentile ranks) onto class size for studies that were well controlled and poorly controlled in the assignment of pupils to classes (from Glass and Smith, 1979).

crete and useful. These advantages should motivate future efforts to include, wherever possible, an examination of interactions as well as main effects.

Consider some illustrations. Raudenbush (1983) reviews 18 experiments examining the influence of teachers' expectations on students' IQ. He argues that a summary of main effects is useless because *the treatment varies.* In those studies where teachers knew the children before researchers experimentally influenced expectations, the treatment effect is very weak—close to zero. In studies where teachers were meeting children for the first time, manipulating expectations had a modestly large and consistent effect. Raudenbush concludes that overall statements about expectancy are worth little; how expectations are manipulated becomes the crucial point.

Williams and colleagues (1982) review studies of children's leisure-time television-viewing habits and their school achievement. This topic has been debated for some years. Frequently, arguments are expressed in terms of main effects—television is harmful to children's performance in school, or it is not. Williams and her coauthors demonstrate that it is not so simple. Small amounts of viewing (less than 10 hours per week) are not found to be harmful at all; indeed, if anything, there is evidence that small amounts of viewing are associated with *better* performance in school. Frequent viewing, on the other hand, emerges as harmful: the more frequent, the more harmful.

This review turns up another interesting finding. Children with high IQ's seem to suffer more from frequent viewing than children with low IQ's. The reviewers do not speculate why this might happen. But such a finding is just the sort of stimulus that can guide the design of future work.

This review illustrates a constructive general strategy. A main effect is reported as the first finding. Then, special circumstances where the treatment is particularly beneficial or harmful are isolated. Finally, if a treatment has a special effect on particular kinds of people, this is investigated in more detail. This strategy provides useful information to both policymakers and researchers. A policymaker facing difficult management decisions needs to know something about both a program's average impact and under what circumstances it does particularly well or particularly poorly. Managers guiding the evolution and refinement of programs can benefit from detailed information about what works best and what types of people benefit most. For researchers, identifying the most promising set of program features from among a large set of candidates should guide future efforts. They can formally build important interactions into future research designs. They can put their chips on variables that have a reasonable probability of mattering.

A final thought about "what we have learned." The findings reported in this chapter not only illustrate how reviews can enhance our understanding of complex questions—they also underscore the *myth of the single decisive study*. It is seductive to think that, despite dozens of past research efforts with disparate findings, just one new "really good" study would settle the issue. If we could do it "right" just once, we would know *the* answer.

The evidence argues strongly in the opposite direction. What is *the* right way? Any one study will have a particular research design. Will it be the right one? After all, we have seen how much research design matters. Any one study will have a certain type of comparison group, a certain level of treatment implementation, a particular analysis strategy. We have seen how strongly these features influence findings. The advantage of a review is that each study gains a context. Each can be examined in light of all the others. Shifting the emphasis from designing a "decisive" single study to enriching the composite picture is to society's advantage.

## A CHECKLIST FOR EVALUATING REVIEWS

# 6

After completing a research review or examining a review prepared by someone else, scholars and policymakers may find it useful to have a checklist of key questions to ask. We present ten such questions. We believe they are general enough to apply to both scientific and policy research. We suggest why each question is important and how answers can clarify the conclusions of a review.

The ten questions are

1. What is the precise purpose of the review?
2. How were studies selected?
3. Is there publication bias?
4. Are treatments similar enough to combine?
5. Are control groups similar enough to combine?
6. What is the distribution of study outcomes?

7. Are outcomes related to research design?
8. Are outcomes related to characteristics of programs, participants, and settings?
9. Is the unit of analysis similar across studies?
10. What are guidelines for future research?

1. *What is the precise purpose of the review? Are procedures matched to that purpose?* (See Chapter 2.) The way a review is structured should depend upon its purpose. What question is being asked? Policymakers, researchers, and local program managers may have different emphases when preparing or commissioning a review.

Policymakers often face decisions requiring an estimate of average program performance. For example, Blue Cross/Blue Shield must decide whether to offer third-party payments for psychological treatment. A regulator might judge that extreme detail is not crucial. The key issue is: "On the average, does psychological counseling help people?" Researchers may feel this is too broad a question. But a policymaker's main concern is not with arranging perfect matches between psychologist and client. It is with the overriding policy question of whether therapy services should or should not be reimbursed.

Researchers might come at the problem differently. They might judge that averaging across different mental health programs, with very different types of clients, misses the main objective. The more important questions here become: What kind of counseling is usually best? What sorts of clients benefit most from what types of counseling? Researchers will not be surprised if a particular treatment or program does not work for everyone. Indeed it is often a positive finding to discover that a certain treatment works for *anyone.* So a researcher frequently wants to go beyond "does it work on the average" to questions of what works, how much, and for whom. Knowing something on the average may be important for immediate policy action. But researchers generally undertake reviews to enhance understanding of *why* a program is particularly effective, or *how* it works for certain people. In the long term, such findings benefit policy.

Local program managers may have yet a different emphasis. They are interested in the question of what treatment is best for whom. But they want an additional answer from research findings: they want to know about *feasibility*. Can an experimental treatment be implemented successfully in specific, real-world locales? It is one thing to learn from controlled experimental field trials that highly structured curricula lead to big gains for poorly prepared children while better-prepared children flourish more with less structured curricula. It is quite another thing to build this finding into practice. It requires figuring out which of the children entering a program are poorly prepared. It requires convincing families that the local program manager's judgment is reasonable. It requires dealing with the consequences of assigning some children to one program and different children to another when, as time passes, parents and teachers react to the differences. So a local manager will want to know what works best in theory, but any concrete evidence about what it takes to implement a program successfully will be particularly valuable. A review undertaken for this purpose will have its own special flavor.

Recall that different questions suggest different reviewing strategies. Answering an "on the average" question implies searching for *main effects*. Other questions imply searching for particular *interactions*. Effect-size averaging is most helpful when searching for overall answers. Quantitative techniques for explaining variation are most helpful when a review is undertaken to find particular programs that match well with particular kinds of recipients. Detailed qualitative information becomes particularly important in reviews targeted to answer a manager's questions about feasibility—can a particular experimental treatment be implemented successfully?

2. *How are studies chosen for inclusion? Are selection criteria stated? Are implications of those criteria clear?* (See

Chapter 2.) A systematic search of available literature can yield dozens, even hundreds, of studies. Each becomes a candidate for inclusion in a review. Any review should give the criteria used to choose studies.

What are the options? One extreme is to include all available studies. The argument in favor is that critics might view any exclusion as arbitrary, so it is better to include everything. Casting a wide net will enhance exploratory reviews, where the goal is to identify interesting trends and get a broad flavor of findings. But the net should not be cast foolishly wide. Few reviewers would argue for including a study with fundamental flaws, such as obvious statistical miscalculations. In such cases, the reviewer should make clear the reason for exclusion, and how it might affect overall conclusions.

A second option is to select a stratified sample of studies. Divide studies by research design, and take a sample of each kind. For example, a reviewer may want to ensure inclusion of some randomized experiments, some observational studies, and some sample surveys. This is one way of reducing the labor in a review facing an enormous number of studies.

A third option is to include only published studies. Studies in refereed journals are more likely to have good research designs than similar efforts that "could not get published." So restricting a review to published studies gives one form of quality control. One argument against this strategy is that some good studies never are submitted to refereed journals. Do we want to ignore such work entirely? Another is that journal referees and editors are unenthusiastic about publishing statistically nonsignificant findings, even from well-done studies. Therefore, in a review of a topic where publication bias is suspected, including doctoral theses and unpublished research reports can provide a more balanced perspective.

A fourth option is to use a panel of outside experts. It is rare for one person, no matter how well informed, to know all the literature in a research area. This is especially true for unpublished articles. An outside group of advisors can "nominate" a list of studies using a specific criteria. For example, they may identify some that are particularly strong methodologically. They may identify some that are frequently cited. Or they may choose those that are especially relevant to policy. Outside experts can make the original nominations, or they can supplement a list of studies prepared by the reviewer. The U.S. General Accounting Office has found panels of experts especially useful when synthesizing evaluations of federal programs.

Whatever the rule for choosing studies, a review should say what it was and why it was chosen. Ideally, each review should also discuss the implications of the selection process. Is the sample of studies representative of most work done in the area? If certain kinds of studies were excluded, why were they? Do the included studies have especially large or small samples? This information is important to readers who want to generalize findings to special populations or circumstances.

3. *Is there publication bias?* (See Chapters 2, 3, and 5.) Research studies in many fields are more likely to be published in professional journals if they turn up statistically significant findings. This implies that if a review includes only published articles, one should suspect a bias toward large or statistically significant effects. A reviewer may mistakenly conclude that a program works better on average than the full set of published and unpublished studies would indicate. A good reviewer should make a reasonable effort to see if such bias exists. If it does, any conclusions or inferences must take it into account.

Two concrete steps may help in dealing with this bias. One is to make a serious effort to locate research findings that are not in journals. Such findings may come from chapters in books, research reports from private organizations and government agencies, masters and doctoral theses, and conference papers. A second concrete step is to estimate the extent of any publication bias. This can be done using graphics (see the funnel procedure in Chapter 3), or by comparing a summary measure such as effect size for published versus unpublished studies. Smith (1980) has shown empirically that average effect sizes are usually smaller for unpublished studies than for published studies. Each review should make this same comparison.

The broad idea is that whatever the bundle of findings, they are supposed to represent fairly all the research on that topic. If evidence of publication bias turns up, a reviewer is obligated to incorporate this fact into both statistical summaries and substantive interpretations. This often will mean toning down enthusiasm for positive findings when their only source is a handful of published, statistically significant studies.

4. *Have treatment groups in different studies been examined to see if they are similar in fact as well as in name?* (See Chapters 2, 3, and 4.) A review should explore whether treatments called by the same name in different studies are really the same. Narrative information becomes particularly useful here. A reviewer can often cull from written narratives the details of what went on. For example, for multisite job training programs the reviewer can ask for each site: How many hours a day were spent in classroom activities? Were participants paid while in training? Does the training site have a formal placement service? The reviewer must then make a judgment of whether different studies of job training actually studied the same thing.

Sometimes there is a good chance a priori that similarly labeled treatments will differ across studies. For example, Public Law 94-142, which mandates special services for handicapped children, specifically encourages the formation of "individual educational plans." These plans are structured uniquely for each child. So one can assume when reviewing reports on the effects of 94-142 that the individual studies are not looking at exactly the same treatment.

At the other extreme, sometimes it is quite safe to consider treatments in various studies very similar, and perhaps identical. For example, take a review of studies assessing a specific dose of a drug, such as a five-grain aspirin tablet. We can assume a priori that the drug is the same across the studies. It is true that different manufacturing processes might be represented in different studies, or that different quality-control standards might be used by different manufacturers. But for most practical purposes a five-grain aspirin tablet is a five-grain aspirin tablet, whether given in Massachusetts in 1983 or in California in 1985.

When treatments are not obviously comparable, quantitative comparisons can help a reviewer to see if similarly named treatments are really similar. We suggest concrete quantitative procedures in Chapter 3. This should be supplemented with qualitative analysis of program characteristics, as discussed in Chapter 4. If substantial differences emerge, simple combining is risky. Including studies with different treatments in a single large review raises the question of whether these different treatments produce similar effects. This question must be answered empirically.

5. *Have control groups in different studies been examined for similarities and differences?* (See Chapter 4.) This question applies only to comparative studies. Just as it is important to ask whether a certain treatment was actually similar across a group of studies, a reviewer must ask the same question about control groups. When some studies show a treatment group outperforming the controls while others show no difference, the reviewer asks why. One possible explanation is that control groups in various studies are fundamentally different.

How might control groups differ? One way is that studies may have different experimental designs. Some studies may have randomly assigned people to treatment and control groups, while others may have allowed participants to choose a treatment on their own. Studies where participants are allowed to choose may have selection problems; different kinds of people may choose the treatment rather than the control group. So the control groups in these studies will differ from those where people were randomly assigned.

A second way control groups can differ is in how the researchers define them. Some studies compare a new treatment to a "control" that is no treatment at all. Other studies compare a new treatment to a "control" that is an old or standard or existing treatment. Still other studies compare a new treatment to "controls" that are really alternative new treatments. In each of these circumstances there is a clear comparison group, but the group's fundamental purpose varies.

An example of these different definitions comes from the daycare literature. Ruopp and colleagues (1979) examined many studies of a program called "developmental day care." They found at least four different kinds of control groups: children cared for full time by a parent at home; children in nursery school; children in less costly care called "custodial daycare"; and children cared for in a private home by an adult other than their parent. Simply aggregating findings across these four kinds of comparative studies may not make sense. The results turn out to depend heavily upon which kind of comparison group was used.

6. *What is the distribution of study outcomes?* (See Chapter 3.) It would be remarkable if each of 30 independent studies evaluating a new drug for high blood pressure found that it brought pressure down by exactly 10 systolic units. Indeed, it would be more than remarkable: it would be suspect. Some chance variation among findings is expected.

Usually reviewers have the opposite problem. Many research reviews flounder because individual studies give highly discrepant results. A productive initial step in quantitative analysis is searching for orderly patterns of results. Probably the easiest way to do this is with a simple graph. Plotting study outcomes on the $x$ axis, and their frequency on the $y$ axis, can offer surprisingly rich insights (see Chapter 3).

First, if treatments are really similar, the graph should be well behaved. It should not be especially skewed or asymmetric. Ideally, it should look approximately like a normal distribution, suggesting that differences among findings are probably due to sampling error. If outcomes look grossly irregular, a reviewer must question whether all studies come from the same population. For example, a bimodal distribution indicates that a group of studies might come from two populations. The challenge for a reviewer is to identify the factors that divide studies into the two groups.

Second, a graph should make outliers become noticeable. These extreme observations may or may not bother a reviewer, depending upon the purpose of the review. If its purpose is to identify a typical or central value, a few scattered outliers carry no special information. But if its purpose is to spot the rare failure of a new drug, or a new curriculum that works especially well, identifying outliers can be the most important part of the entire process.

After finding outliers that seem important, the reviewer must look for explanations. Why might this have happened? Is it a consistent or a chance finding? Suppose a group of studies of heart bypass surgery have a small cluster of particularly successful reports. Then the big question is whether they share any special feature. Perhaps the exceptionally successful studies all involved younger patients. Perhaps they were all done at large urban hospitals with exceptional facilities. There are usually a large number of possible explanations. Finding a convincing reason to choose any one is a real challenge. This brings home the enormous value of successfully combining substantive and technical knowledge in reviews. It is easy enough to graph outcomes and spot outliers. It is much harder to identify what features distinguish the exceptional studies from the others.

7. *Does the review relate findings from different studies to type of research design?* (See Chapters 2, 3, 4, and 5.) We reported in Chapter 5 that many reviews find a relation between a study's findings and its research design. Sometimes this relation is very strong (Chalmers, 1982). All reviews, whether statistical or narrative, should search for such a relationship. Finding it will often explain otherwise contradictory outcomes.

An extreme case illustrates what we can learn. Suppose a

review of job training studies turns up a small number of positive findings together with many indicating no success. Then the simplest conclusion is that the evidence is mixed. Job training seems to work occasionally. Indeed this conclusion might be correct. But now we introduce information about study design. The review has 50 studies. Ten randomly assigned people to programs; 40 did not. Suppose the 10 randomized designs show clearly positive findings and the 40 nonrandomized efforts show little success. This can be valuable information.

First, it suggests that job training may be far more beneficial than commonly reported. After all, the subset of well-controlled studies shows positive effects, although these are the minority of studies altogether.

Second, it tells us that certain procedures for carrying out a review, such as averaging of effect sizes (see Chapter 3), should be used very cautiously. If information about research design is not included, any "on the average" findings can swamp the positive findings from the few well-designed studies.

A third reason for relating results to design is to guide future work. If different designs lead to conflicting results, scientists must ask why. Even if we cannot discover the answer, simply knowing that a relationship exists should make us cautious about relying on only one type of study.

8. *Does the review relate outcomes to different features of* (a) *programs,* (b) *participants, and* (c) *settings?* (See Chapters 2, 3, 4, and 5.) A common goal of reviews is to report broad findings, such as "the treatment works" or "the treatment fails." While sometimes this is adequate, a review ideally should tell us more: *What* constitutes a successful program? *For whom* is it most and least effective? *In what settings* does it work best? Quantitative procedures offer systematic ways to search for answers. Qualitative information and case studies are particularly useful for identifying special circumstances that might get lost in purely numerical analyses.

A review's value will increase sharply if it helps readers to answer "matching" questions. What program is best for what recipient in a given circumstance? Answering such matching questions is precisely where a collection of findings has its comparative advantage over a single study. It is hard for one study to examine systematically all interesting program features, participant characteristics, and program settings. Combining findings from many studies makes it possible to look across many different combinations of program, recipients, and settings to see what works best.

A good review does more than just extend the range of background variables. Certain questions can be answered *only* by looking across several studies. For example, suppose a reviewer is examining many studies of the effectiveness of preschools, each of which looks at one site. The reviewer will probably find some factors that vary within each site. An example is age of the children, or family income. Other features will have no within-site variation. For example, per-pupil expenditure is the same for every child in a certain preschool. So are geographical location and staff-to-child ratio. These constant features produce *contextual* effects.

A good review should see if differences in an outcome (such as reading performance) relate to contextual differences. Such differences are often the part of the curriculum most easily manipulated. Additional examples of contextual factors in preschool are total group size and the presence or absence of programmed instruction materials.

The only way to estimate the influence of a contextual feature is to look at a *group* of studies. This is because a contextual feature has no variation in any one study—its value is the same for each participant. It is possible to examine the importance of such features only when they vary from place to place. To investigate the importance of per-pupil expenditure, we must find some studies with high expenditures and others with low expenditures. Only a review permits this.

9. *Do studies use similar units of analysis?* (See Chapters 2 and 3.) In an ideal world, each study would give detailed information about each participant. This would enable a reader

to recompute existing findings and try new ideas for analysis. But in the real world raw data rarely appear. Most studies provide only summary information.

A reviewer then faces a dilemma. Can we tell from short summaries whether findings are comparable? One step toward answering this question is to identify the *unit of analysis* for each study. Some studies will focus on individual people. Others will use aggregated units, such as classrooms or hospitals. When studies use different units of analysis their summary statistics can be difficult to reconcile.

Suppose, for example, a reviewer is tackling several regression analyses where predicting a student's achievement is the goal. Predictor variables include some that are controllable (the size of a class; the number of hours of school per week) and some that are uncontrollable (student's age, or sex, or family income). A summary report from each study gives the regression coefficients and $R^2$.

Assume the $R^2$'s are different across studies. It is appropriate to compare them directly only when the unit of analysis is the same for each regression. If units of analysis differ, it would not be surprising to find wide variation in $R^2$ values. Usually, the more aggregated the data, the higher the $R^2$ will be (see Chapter 2). For example, the National Day Care Study (Ruopp et al., 1979) analyzed the *same data set* in two ways. Analyses using classroom mean scores yielded $R^2$ values more than twice as high as analyses using individual children's scores.

Any review comparing summary statistics should identify the unit of analysis for each study. For example, a group of medical reports examining a surgical procedure might well include studies analyzing individual patients, others looking at hospital averages, and still others based on physicians' caseloads. A simple list of $R^2$ values could therefore display enormous variability. Tying each $R^2$ value to the unit of analysis underlying it might explain much of the variation.

10. *Does the review offer guidance for designing future studies?* (See Chapter 4.) A major purpose of reviews is to

suggest to the designer of the eleventh study what can be learned from the first ten. Reviews can provide such guidance in at least two ways.

First, a review can help by identifying the most promising experimental manipulations and comparisons. Given finite resources, it is not possible to build all variables formally into each new effort. A review can examine a large number of possible variables that might be important, and eliminate many of them as serious candidates for new research. If hospital size is not related to surgical success in ten well-done studies, it is unlikely to pop up as crucial in the eleventh. Using prior reviews to reduce the number of experimental variables should improve the statistical power and guide the allocation of resources in a new study.

Second, a review can help a researcher to choose between organizing one big new effort at a single site and organizing a series of small efforts at many sites. Suppose funds are available to evaluate a new job training program involving 1000 trainees. Is it better to conduct one study with all 1000 trainees at one site, or to carry out five smaller studies in different places with 200 trainees each? Existing research can guide this decision. On the one hand, suppose past evaluations show little variation in the success of job training across different settings. Then the wisest decision probably is to focus the entire new effort at one site. The large sample size will help to identify subtle ways in which the new program differs from current practice. On the other hand, suppose a review of earlier findings shows the value of job training to vary widely across sites. Then it could be a mistake to focus on one particular setting. Setting-by-treatment interactions should be expected. This expectation can only be assessed by trying the new program in several places.

The particular guidance a research review provides will differ from one substantive area to another. These examples illustrate the benefits of designing into new research the messages of the old. The implication for reviewers is that simply concluding with the usual "more research is needed" is not enough. Reviewers must make a conscious effort to identify what specific directions new initiatives should take. This linking of past and present is crucial if research is to achieve its full potential for enhancing both science and policy.

# REFERENCES

Ad Hoc Coalition on Block Grants. 1981. *Block grants briefing book*. Washington, D.C.

Adler, R., G. Lesser, L. Meringoff, T. Robertson, J. Rossiter, S. Ward, B. Friedlander, and L. Isler. 1980. *The effects of television advertising on children*. Lexington, MA: Lexington Books.

Andrews, G., B. Guitar, and P. Howie. 1980. Meta-analysis of the effects of stuttering treatment. *Journal of Speech and Hearing Disorders, 45,* 287–307.

Astin, A. A., and S. Ross. 1960. Glutamic acid and human intelligence. *Psychological Bulletin, 57,* 429–434.

Bailey, W. C. 1966. Correctional outcome: an evaluation of 100 reports. *Journal of Criminal Law, Criminology, and Police Science, 57,* 153–160.

Baker, K., and A. de Kanter. 1982. Federal policy and the effectiveness of bilingual education. Manuscript. U.S. Department of Education.

REFERENCES

Bearman, J. E., R. B. Loewenson, and W. H. Gullen. 1974. *Muench's postulates, laws, and corollaries, or biometricians' views on clinical studies.* Biometrics Note no. 4. Bethesda, MD: Office of Biometry and Epidemiology, National Eye Institute, National Institutes of Health.

Belsky, J., and L. D. Steinberg. 1978. The effects of day care: a critical review. *Child Development, 49,* 929–949.

Bissell, J. 1970. The cognitive effects of preschool programs for disadvantaged children. Ed.D. dissertation, Graduate School of Education, Harvard University.

Boruch, R. F., and D. C. Cordray. 1981. An appraisal of educational program evaluations: federal, state, and local agencies. Report to the U.S. Department of Education, contract no. 300-79-0467. Evanston, IL: Northwestern University.

Burger, J. M. 1981. Motivational biases in the attribution of responsibility for an accident: a meta-analysis of the defensive-attribution hypothesis. *Psychological Bulletin, 90,* 496–512.

Campbell, D. T. 1975. Degrees of freedom and the case study. *Comparative Political Studies, 8,* 178–193.

Campbell, D. T., and J. Stanley. 1966. *Experimental and quasi-experimental designs for research.* Chicago: Rand McNally.

Canner, P. L., Y. B. Huang, and C. L. Meinert. 1981a. On the detection of outlier clinics in medical and surgical trials. I. Practical considerations. *Controlled Clinical Trials, 2,* 231–240.

—— 1981b. On the detection of outlier clinics in medical and surgical trials. II. Theoretical considerations. *Controlled Clinical Trials, 2,* 241–252.

Chalmers, T. C. 1982. The randomized controlled trial as a basis for therapeutic decisions. In J. M. Lachin, N. Tygstrup, and E. Juhl, eds., *The randomized clinical trial and therapeutic decisions.* New York: Marcel Dekker.

Cliff, N. 1959. Adverbs as multipliers. *Psychological Review, 66,* 27.

Cohen, J. 1977. *Statistical power analysis for the behavioral sciences.* Rev. ed. New York: Academic Press.

Coleman, J. S. 1966. *Equality of educational opportunity.* Washington, D.C.: U.S. Government Printing Office.

Cook, T. D., and L. C. Leviton. 1980. Reviewing the literature: a comparison of traditional methods with meta-analysis. *Journal of Personality, 48,* 449–472.

Cooper, H. M. 1979. Statistically combining independent studies: a meta-analysis of sex differences in conformity research. *Journal of Personality and Social Psychology, 37,* 131–146.

Cooper, H. M., and R. Rosenthal. 1980. Statistical versus traditional procedures for summarizing research findings. *Psychological Bulletin, 87,* 442–449.

DerSimonian, R., and N. M. Laird. 1983. Evaluating the effect of coaching on SAT scores: a meta-analysis. *Harvard Educational Review, 53,* 1–15.

Devine, E. C., and T. D. Cook. 1983. Effects of psycho-educational interventions on length of hospital stay: a meta-analytic review of 34 studies. In *Evaluation Studies Review Annual,* vol. 8, ed. R. J. Light. Beverly Hills, CA: Sage.

Dukes, W. F. 1965. N = 1. *Psychological Bulletin, 64,* 74–79.

Durlak, J. A. 1979. Comparative effectiveness of paraprofessional and professional helpers. *Psychological Bulletin, 86,* 80–92.

Eagly, A. H., and L. L. Carli. 1981. Sex of researchers and sexed-typed communications as determinants of sex differences in influenceability: a meta-analysis of social influence studies. *Psychological Bulletin, 90,* 1–20.

Fienberg, S., and P. Grambsch. 1979. An assessment of the accuracy of "The effectiveness of correctional treatment." In L. Sechrest, S. White, and E. Brown, eds., *The rehabilitation of criminal offenders: problems and prospects,* Appendix. Washington, D.C.: National Academy of Sciences Press.

Fisher, R. A. 1935. *The design of experiments.* Edinburgh: Oliver and Boyd.

Fosburg, S., and F. Glantz. 1981. Analysis plan for the Child Care Food Program. Submitted to the Food and Nutrition Service, U.S. Department of Agriculture, by Abt Associates Inc., Cambridge, MA.

Francis, I. 1967. Inference in the classification problem. Ph.D. dissertation, Harvard University.

Franseth, J., and R. Koury. 1966. *Survey of research on grouping as related to pupil learning.* Washington, D.C.: U.S. Government Printing Office.

Freeman, F. N., K. J. Holzinger, and B. C. Mitchell. 1928. The influence of environment on the intelligence, school achievement, and conduct of foster children. *National Society of Education, 27,* pt. 1, 367–384.

Freeman, R. 1971. *The market for college trained manpower: a study in the economics of career choice.* Cambridge, MA: Harvard University Press.

Ghez, G., and M. Grossman. 1979. Preventive care, care for children, and national health insurance. Paper presented at the American Enterprise Institute Conference: National Health Insurance: What Now, What Later, What Never?, Washington, D.C., Oct. 4–5.

Gilbert, J. P., R. J. Light, and F. Mosteller. 1975. Assessing social innovation: an empirical base for policy. In C. A. Bennett and A. A. Lumsdaine, eds., *Evaluation and experiment.* New York: Academic Press.

Gilbert, J. P., B. McPeek, and F. Mosteller. 1977. Progress in surgery and anesthesia: benefits and risks of innovation therapy. In J. Bunker, B. Barnes, and F. Mosteller, eds., *Costs, risks and benefits of surgery.* New York: Oxford University Press.

Glass, G. V. 1976. Primary, secondary, and meta-analysis of research. *Educational Researcher, 6,* 3–8.

——— 1977. Integrating findings: the meta-analysis of research. *Review of Research in Education, 5,* 351–379.

——— 1978. Bibliography of writings on the integration of research findings: the meta-analysis of research. Manuscript, Laboratory of Educational Research, University of Colorado.

Glass, G. V., B. McGaw, and M. L. Smith. 1981. *Meta-analysis of social research.* Beverly Hills, CA: Sage.

Glass, G. V., and M. L. Smith. 1979. Meta-analysis of research on class size and achievement. *Educational Evaluation and Policy Analysis, 1,* 2–16.

Gottman, J. J., and G. V. Glass. 1978. Analysis of interrupted time-series experiments. In T. R. Kratochwill, ed., *Single subject research.* New York: Academic Press.

Gould, S. J. 1981. *The mismeasurement of man.* New York: Norton.

Greenwald, A. G. 1975. Consequences of prejudice against the null hypothesis. *Psychological Bulletin, 82,* 1–20.

Hall, J. A. 1978. Gender effects of decoding nonverbal cues. *Psychological Bulletin, 85,* 845–857.

Haney, W. 1974. Units of analysis issues in the evaluation of Project Follow Through. Document prepared for U.S. Office of Education, contract no. OEC-0-74-0394. Cambridge, MA: Huron Institute.

Harris, B. 1979. Whatever happened to Little Albert? *American Psychologist, 34,* 151–160.

—— 1980. Ceremonial versus critical history of psychology. *American Psychologist, 35,* 218–219.

Harvard Child Health Project. 1977. *Report of the Harvard Child Health Project Task Force.* Cambridge, MA: Ballinger.

Hedges, L. V. 1982. Estimation of effect size from a series of independent experiments. *Psychological Bulletin, 92,* 490–499.

Hedges, L. V., and I. Olkin. 1980. Vote-counting methods in research synthesis. *Psychological Bulletin, 88,* 359–369.

Heller, K., W. H. Holtzman, and S. Messick, eds. 1982. *Placing children in special education: a strategy for equity.* Washington, D.C.: National Academy of Sciences Press.

Herriot, R. E. 1978. Federal initiatives and rural school improvements. Findings from the Experimental School Program, prepared for the National Institute of Education by Abt Associates Inc., Cambridge, MA, March.

Herson, M., and D. H. Barlow. 1976. *Single-case experimental designs: strategies for studying behavior change.* New York: Pergamon.

Hoaglin, D. C., R. J. Light, B. McPeek, F. Mosteller, and M. A. Stoto. 1982. *Data for decisions.* Cambridge, MA: Abt Books.

Hood, R., and R. Sparks. 1970. *Key issues in criminology.* New York: McGraw-Hill.

Hunter, J. E., F. L. Schmidt, and G. B. Jackson. 1982. *Meta-analysis: cumulating research findings across studies.* Beverly Hills, CA: Sage.

Jackson, G. B. 1980. Methods for integrative reviews. *Review of Educational Research, 50,* 438–460.

Jencks, C. 1972. *Inequality: a reassessment of the effect of family and schooling in America.* New York: Basic Books.

Jensen, A. R. 1969. How much can we boost IQ and scholastic achievement? *Harvard Educational Review, 39,* 1–123.

Johnson, D. W., G. Maruyama, R. Johnson, D. Nelson, and L. Skon. 1981. Effects of cooperative, competitive, and individualistic goal structures on achievement: a meta-analysis. *Psychological Bulletin, 89,* 47–62.

Jones, R. R., M. R. Weinrott, and R. S. Vaught. 1978. Effects of social dependency on the agreement between visual and statistical inference. *Journal of Applied Behavior Analysis, 11,* 277–283.

Kamin, L. J. 1974. *The science and politics of IQ.* Potomac, MD: Erlbaum.

———— 1978. Comment on Munsinger's review of adoption studies. *Psychological Bulletin, 85,* 194–201.

Kennedy, M. M. 1979. Generalizing from single case studies. *Evaluation Quarterly, 3,* 661–678.

Kippel, G. 1981. Identifying exceptional schools. *New Directions for Program Evaluation, 11,* 83–100.

Kissinger. H. A. 1960. *The necessity for choice: prospects of American foreign policy.* New York: Harper and Row.

Klitgaard, R. E. 1978. Identifying exceptional performers. *Policy Analysis,* Fall, 529–547.

Klitgaard, R. E., S. Dadabhoy, and S. Litkouhi. 1979. Cognitive equality and educational policies: an example from Pakistan. *Pakistan Development Review, 18,* 79–88.

———— 1981. Regression without a model. *Policy Sciences, 13,* 99–115.

Klitgaard, R. E., and G. Hall. 1973. *A statistical search for unusually effective schools.* Santa Monica, CA: Rand Corporation. Rpt. in W. Fairley and F. Mosteller, eds., *Statistics and public policy.* Reading, MA: Addison-Wesley, 1977.

Kratochwill, T. R. 1977. N = 1: an alternative research strategy for school psychologists. *Journal of School Psychology, 15,* 239–249.

———— 1978. *Single subject research.* New York: Academic Press.

Kuhn, T. S. 1962. *The structure of scientific revolutions:* Chicago: University of Chicago Press.

Kulik, C. C., and J. A. Kulik. 1982. Effects of ability grouping on secondary school students: a meta-analysis of evaluation findings. *American Educational Research Journal, 19,* 415–428.

Kulik, J. A., C. C. Kulik, and P. A. Cohen. 1979. A meta-analysis of outcome studies of Keller's personalized system of instruction. *American Psychologist, 34,* 307–318.

Lazar, I., and R. Darlington. 1978. Lasting effects after preschool. Manuscript, Department of Human Services, Cornell University.

Leifer, A., N. Gordon, and S. Graves. 1974. Children's television: more than mere entertainment. *Harvard Educational Review, 44,* 213–245.

Lesser, G. S. 1974. *Children and television.* New York: Vintage Books.

Leviton, L. C., and T. D. Cook. 1981. What differentiates meta-analysis from other forms of review. *Journal of Personality, 49,* 231–236.

Lewis, C. E., A. Lorimer, C. Lindesman, B. B. Palmer, and M. A. Lewis. 1974. An evaluation of the impact of school nurse practitioners. *Journal of School Health, 44,* 331–335.

Light, R. J. 1979. Capitalizing on variation: how conflicting research findings can be helpful for policy. *Educational Researcher, 8*(8), 3–8.

———— 1980. Synthesis methods: some judgment calls that must be made. *Evaluation in Education: an International Review Series, 4,* 18–21.

Light, R. J., and D. B. Pillemer. 1982. Numbers and narrative: combining their strengths in research reviews. *Harvard Educational Review, 52,* 1–26.

Light, R. J., and P. V. Smith. 1971. Accumulating evidence: procedures for resolving contradictions among different studies. *Harvard Educational Review, 41,* 429–471.

Lipton, D., R. Martinson, and J. Wilks. 1975. The effectiveness of correctional treatment: a survey of treatment evaluation studies. New York: Praeger.

Maccoby, E. E., and C. N. Jacklin. 1974. *The psychology of sex differences.* Stanford, CA: Stanford University Press.

Mahoney, M. J. 1976. *Scientist as subject.* Cambridge, MA: Ballinger.

McClintock, C. C., D. Brannon, and S. Maynard-Moody. 1979. Applying the logic of sample surveys to qualitative case studies: the case cluster method. *Administrative Science Quarterly, 24,* 612–629.

McCulloch, T. L. 1950. The effect of glutamic acid feeding on cognitive abilities of institutionalized mental defectives. *American Journal of Mental Deficiency, 55,* 117–122.

Meehl, P. E. 1965. Seer over sign: the first good example. *Journal of Experimental Research in Personality, 1,* 27–32.

Merenstein, J. H., H. Wolfe, and K. M. Barker. 1974. The use of nurse practitioners in a general practice. *Medical Care, 12,* 445–452.

Miller, G. A. 1956. The magical number seven, plus or minus two: some limits on our capacity for processing information. *Psychological Review, 63,* 81–97.

Mollica, R. F. 1983. From asylum to community: the threatened disintegration of public psychiatry. *New England Journal of Medicine, 308,* 367–372.

Mondale, W. 1971. Address given to the American Educational Research Association's annual meeting, New York, Feb.

Mosteller, F. 1976. Swine flu: quantifying the "possibility." *Science, 192,* 1286–1288.

Mosteller, F., and R. R. Bush. 1954. Selected quantitative techniques. In G. Lindzey, ed., *Handbook of social psychology: theory and method,* vol. 1. Cambridge, MA: Addison-Wesley.

Mosteller, F., and D. Wallace. 1964. *Inference and disputed authorship: The Federalist.* Reading, MA: Addison-Wesley.

Munsinger, H. 1974. The adopted child's IQ: a critical review. *Psychological Bulletin, 82,* 623–659.

———— 1978. Reply to Kamin. *Psychological Bulletin, 85,* 202–206.

Murray, C. A., and L. A. Cox, Jr. 1979. *Beyond probation: juvenile corrections and the chronic delinquent.* Beverly Hills, CA: Sage.

Parlett, M., and D. Hamilton. 1976. Evaluation as illumination: a new approach to the study of innovatory programs. In *Evaluation Studies Review Annual,* vol. 1, ed. G. V. Glass. Beverly Hills, CA: Sage.

Particle Data Group. 1976. Reviews of particle properties. *Reviews of Modern Physics, 48,* S1–S20.

Patton, M. Q. 1975. *Alternative evaluation research paradigm.* Grand Forks, ND: University of North Dakota Press, for the North Dakota Study Group on Evaluation.

———— 1980. *Qualitative evaluation methods.* Beverly Hills, CA: Sage.

Pflaum, S. W., H. J. Walberg, M. Karegianes, and S. P. Rasher. 1980. Reading instruction: a quantitative analysis. *Educational Researcher, 9,* 12–18.

Pillemer, D. B., and R. J. Light. 1979. Using the results of randomized experiments to construct social programs: three caveats. In *Evaluation Studies Review Annual,* vol. 4. ed. L. Sechrest. Beverly Hills, CA: Sage.

———— 1980a. Benefiting from variation in study outcomes. *New Directions for Methodology of Social and Behavioral Science, 5,* 1–12.

———— 1980b. Synthesizing outcomes: how to use research evidence from many studies. *Harvard Educational Review, 50,* 176–195.

Raudenbush, S. W. 1983. Utilizing controversy as a source of hypotheses for meta-analysis: the case of teacher expectancy's effect on pupil IQ. In *Evaluation Studies Review Annual,* vol. 8, ed. R. J. Light. Beverly Hills, CA: Sage.

Reichardt, C. S., and T. D. Cook. 1979. Beyond qualitative *versus* quantitative methods. In T. D. Cook and C. S. Reichardt, eds., *Qualitative and quantitative methods in evaluation research.* Beverly Hills, CA: Sage.

Rein, M., and S. H. White. 1977. Can policy research help policy? *Public Interest,* Fall, 119–136.

Rosenthal, R. 1978. Combining results of independent studies. *Psychological Bulletin, 85,* 185–193.

———— 1980. Summarizing significance levels. *New Directions for Methodology of Social and Behavioral Science, 5,* 33–46.

———— 1983. Assessing the statistical and social importance of the effects of psychotherapy. *Journal of Consulting and Clinical Psychology, 51,* 4–13.

Rosenthal, R., and L. Jacobson. 1968. *Pygmalion in the classroom.* New York: Holt, Rinehart and Winston.

Rosenthal, R., and D. B. Rubin. 1978. Interpersonal expectancy effects: the first 345 studies. *Behavioral and Brain Sciences, 3,* 377–415.

———— 1982a. A simple, general purpose display of magnitude of experimental effect. *Journal of Educational Psychology, 74,* 166–169.

———— 1982b. Comparing effect sizes of independent studies. *Psychological Bulletin, 92,* 500–504.

———— 1982c. Further meta-analytic procedures for assessing cognitive gender differences. *Journal of Educational Psychology, 74,* 708–712.

Ruopp, R., J. Travers, F. Glantz, and C. Coelen. 1979. *Children at the center: report of the National Day Care Study.* Cambridge, MA: Abt Books.

Salter, W. J. 1980. Conducting social program evaluations. Essay prepared for Bolt, Beranek, and Newman, Inc., Cambridge, MA, Aug.

Schank, R. C., and R. P. Abelson. 1977. *Scripts, plans, goals, and understanding.* Hillsdale, N.J.: Erlbaum.

REFERENCES

Schneider, J. A., N. J. Stevens, and L. G. Tornatzky. 1982. Policy research and analysis: an empirical profile, 1975–1980. *Policy Sciences, 15,* 99–114.

Scriven, M. 1966. Causes, connections and conditions in history. In W. H. Dray, ed., *Philosophical analysis and history.* New York: Harper and Row.

Sechrest, L., S. White, and E. Brown, eds. 1979. *The rehabilitation of criminal offenders: problems and prospects.* Washington, D.C.: National Academy of Sciences Press.

Seligman, M. E. P. 1971. Phobias and preparedness. *Behavioral Therapy, 2,* 307–320.

Selvidge, J. 1972. Assigning probabilities to rare events. Ph.D. dissertation, Harvard University.

Shadish, W. R. 1982. A review and critique of controlled studies of the effectiveness of preventive child health care. *Health Policy Quarterly, 2,* 24–52.

Shonkoff, J. 1982. Biological and social factors contributing to mild mental retardation. In K. Heller, W. H. Holtzman, and S. Messick, eds., *Placing children in special education: a strategy for equity.* Washington, D.C.: National Academy of Sciences Press.

Singer, J. 1983. Hierarchical units in analysis of grouped data. Ph.D. dissertation, Department of Statistics, Harvard University.

Slack, W. V., and D. Porter. 1980. The Scholastic Aptitude Test: a critical appraisal. *Harvard Educational Review, 50,* 154–175.

Smith, M. L. 1980. Publication bias and meta-analysis. *Evaluation in Education, 4,* 22–24.

Smith, M. L., and G. V. Glass. 1977. Meta-analysis of psychotherapy outcome studies. *American Psychologist, 32,* 752–760.

Smith, M. S., and J. Bissell. 1970. The impact of Head Start. *Harvard Educational Review, 40,* 51–104.

Stake, R. E. 1978. The case study method in social inquiry. *Educational Research, 7*(2), 5–8.

Stock, W. A., M. Okun, M. Haring, and R. Witter. 1982. Health and subjective well-being: a meta-analysis. Paper given at the Annual Meeting of the American Gerontological Association, Boston.

Straw, R. B. 1983. Deinstitutionalization in mental health: a meta-analysis. In *Evaluation Studies Review Annual,* vol. 8, ed. R. J. Light. Beverly Hills, CA: Sage.

Szucko, J. J., and B. Kleinmuntz. 1981. Statistical versus clinical lie detection. *American Psychologist, 36,* 488–496.

Tukey, J. W. 1962. The future of data analysis. *Annals of Mathematical Statistics, 33,* 1–67.

U.S. Congressional Budget Office. 1982. *CETA training programs—do they work for adults?* Washington, D.C.: Congressional Budget Office.

U.S. General Accounting Office. 1981. *Disparities still exist in who gets special education.* GAO-IPE-81-1. Washington, D.C.

———— 1982a. *CETA programs for disadvantaged adults: What do we know about their enrollees, services, and effectiveness?* GAO-IPE-82-2. Washington, D.C., June 14.

———— 1982b. *Lessons learned from past block grants: implications for congressional oversight.* GAO-IPE-82-8. Washington, D.C., Sept. 23.

———— 1982c. *The elderly should benefit from expanded home health care but increasing those services will not insure cost reductions.* GAO-IPE-83-1. Washington, D.C., Dec. 7.

Walberg, H. J. 1983. Synthesis of research on teaching. In M. C. Wittrock, ed., *The third handbook of research on teaching.* Washington, D.C.: American Educational Research Association.

Walberg, H. J., and E. H. Haertel. 1980. Research integration: the state of the art. *Evaluation in Education: An International Review Series* (special issue), *4,* 1–142.

Warr, P., and G. Perry. 1982. Paid employment and women's psychological well-being. *Psychological Bulletin, 91,* 498–516.

White, K. R. 1982. The relation between socioeconomic status and academic achievement. *Psychological Bulletin, 91,* 461–481.

Williams, P. A., E. H. Haertel, G. H. Haertel, and H. J. Walberg. 1982. The impact of leisure-time television on school learning: a research synthesis. *American Educational Research Journal, 19,* 19–50.

Willson, V. L., and R. R. Putnam. 1982. A meta-analysis of pretest desensitization effects in experimental design. *American Educational Research Journal, 19,* 249–258.

Wilson, J. Q. 1980. "What works" revisited: new findings on criminal rehabilitation. *Public Interest,* Fall, no. 61, 3–17.

Wortman, P. M. 1982. Meta-analysis: a validity perspective. Paper presented to the Evaluation Research Society, Baltimore, Oct.

**REFERENCES**

Wortman, P. M., and W. H. Yeaton. 1983. Synthesis of results in controlled trials of coronary artery bypass graft surgery. In *Evaluation Studies Review Annual,* vol. 8, ed. R. J. Light. Beverly Hills, CA: Sage.

Yin, R. K., E. Bingham, and K. A. Heald. 1976. The difference that quality makes: the case of literature reviews. *Sociological Methods and Research, 5,* 139–156.

Yin, R. K., and K. A. Heald. 1975. Using the case survey method to analyze policy studies. *Administrative Science Quarterly, 20,* 371–381.

Yin, R. K., and D. Yates. 1974. *Street-level governments: assessing decentralization and urban services.* Santa Monica, CA: Rand Corporation.

Zabrenko, R. N., and D. G. Chambers. 1952. An evaluation of glutamic acid in mental deficiency. *American Journal of Psychiatry, 108,* 881–887.

Zigler, E., and P. K. Trickett. 1978. IQ, social competence, and evaluation of early childhood intervention programs. *American Psychologist, 33,* 789–798.

Zigler, E., and J. Valentine. 1979. *Project Head Start.* New York: Free Press.

Zimiles, H. M. 1980. On making developmental psychology more relevant. *Society for Research in Child Development Newsletter,* Fall.

# INDEX